The Most Common Errors in English Usage And How to Avoid Them

Elaine Bender
El Camino College, Torrance, CA
Pasadena City College, Pasadena, CA

BARNES
&NOBLE
BOOKS
NEW YORK

An American BookWorks Corporation Project.

Copyright © 2003 by American BookWorks Corporation.

This edition published by Barnes & Noble Publishing, Inc.

ISBN 0-7607-4137-9

Printed and bound in the United States of America

MP 9 8 7 6 5 4 3 2

Contents

GRAMMAR RULES—AN INTRODUCTION

What does the title to this Introduction mean? Is it a heading that tells the reader a list of rules will follow? Or is it a complete sentence meaning that grammar controls something? Because the grammar of the title is not clear, this ambiguous phrase means both a list and a statement about grammar.

As a list of rules, grammar governs standard written English. Although we use different conventions when speaking or writing casually, standard written English provides the basis for public communication. It is the language of business, education, and politics. It provides a foundation for more specialized languages used in areas like law and science.

Public communication, written or verbal, leads others to judge us. No one wants to be considered ignorant or uneducated. Therefore, we are concerned about our language. We may worry about whether to use *who* or *whom*. Is it permissible to begin a sentence with *and*? May a sentence end with a preposition? As a list of rules, grammar provides us with a guide to the language used by educated speakers and writers, making us confident we (and our communications) will be judged favorably.

But grammar is more than a list of rules. Grammar controls meaning. Contemporary linguists believe that in humans there is a universal grammar, a way of creating meaning common to all languages. Yet individual languages have different grammars. In English, the usual order of the parts of a sentence is subject-verb-object. In Japanese, it is subject-object-verb. Some language do not use pronouns. Instead, they add a sound or syllable to word to indicate the relationship conveyed in English by a prepositional phrase. The grammar of a particular language provides a pattern of usage that assures that people who use the language will convey what they mean and understand each other.

Meaning is the crucial issue. Effective grammar conveys your meanings clearly and unambiguously and enables to you communicate as efficiently as possible. Such communication is a key to succeeding whenever information exchange is part of a transaction.

Has technology made the process or producing correct written communication easier? It has, and it has not. Certainly, editing a document on a word processor is simpler than the older methods of cutting and pasting and retyping. Some kinds of electronic communication favor shortcuts and abbreviations which do not follow the rules of standard written English. But when your prepare a document to be printed and read—a letter to a client, an assignment for a college course, the text of a speech, a report to the board of directors—standard written English remains your best choice. In this case, electronic aids may mislead you. Spelling checkers will not find the error if you confuse *cause* and *course*. Nor will grammar checkers know if your meaning requires you to write *consistent in* or *consistent with*. Style checkers always flag the use of the passive voice as an error; only you can determine if the sentence requires the passive voice.

This book is designed to help you communicate better by making your language correct and your meaning clear. It uses a functional approach—that is, it is organized in a practical manner, according to the grammatical errors people make most frequently. The text presents important grammatical rules, with examples of correct and incorrect usage, arranged to focus on grammatical practice rather than theory. In this way, the book allows you to isolate the grammatical errors that tend to trap you, locate them in your sentences, and correct them before you produce a final document.

Six Writing Principles to Remember

Chapter 1 discusses parts of speech and the components of the English sentence. It is a quick refresher course in grammatical terms. You'll find references to "conjunctions" and "predicates"—terms you may have known but possibly have forgotten through lack of use. Chapter 1 introduces the vocabulary used for discussing grammar throughout the rest of the text.

Chapters 2 through 8 are organized around six basic writing principles. Keep these principles firmly in mind. They provide the foundation on which all grammatical rules are built:

> Make the parts of a sentence fit together—make sure words agree with each other.
> Keep the time order of events straight.
> Choose the active voice over the passive voice.
> Keep related words close together.
> Show the relationship between ideas clearly.
> Punctuate for meaning.

Make the parts of a sentence fit together—make sure words agree with each other. In grammatical terminology, "agreement" means consistency in forms of words. Chapter 2 deals with agreement by introducing the idea of "case"—the concept that some nouns and pronouns change their form according to the role they play in a sentence (whether they act as subjects or objects). Chapter 3 examines two chief sets of agreement errors: mistakes in subject-verb agreement, and mistakes in pronoun-antecedent agreement.

Keep the time order of events straight. Chapter 4 discusses "tense," or the "time sense" of verbs. There are verb forms to capture actions taking place in every time sequence the human mind can imagine: present, past, future, present progressive, future perfect, and all the others. Whenever you choose verbs, you must be sure their forms express the time sequence you wish to convey.

Prefer the active voice over the passive voice, unless meaning requires the passive. Chapter 5 examines mood and voice and recommends that you select active verbs over passive verbs. The first of these sentences is written in the active voice, the second in the passive: "The sales representative approached the customer." "The customer was approached by the sales representative." As you can see, the active voice is more concise, more direct, and has more energy. It places the sentence's emphasis on the *doer* of the action rather than on the *receiver* of the action.

Keep related words together. In Chapter 6 you will find rules governing the correct use of "modifiers," those words and groups of words that describe or make more exact the meanings of other words. Modifiers generally should be kept short. Further, since modifiers latch themselves onto the nearest substantive word or word group, you must place them carefully in your sentence—as close as possible to the words they modify.

Show the relationship between ideas clearly. Chapter 7 concentrates on connectives—all those miscellaneous words and phrases that make the *connections* between your ideas clear and that therefore provide the logical framework for your sentence or paragraph. Connectives pinpoint the logical relationships in your ideas. They act as the skeletal framework organizing your ideas, and they tell your readers how to connect your ideas in their minds.

Punctuate for meaning. Chapter 8 examines punctuation, with a special emphasis on the comma. The comma is deceptive: It is the most frequently used punctuation mark and the one that causes the greatest number of grammatical difficulties. This chapter focuses on the logic behind comma rules and shows the practical ways those rules control a sentence's meaning.

How to Use This Book

You can use this book in two ways: as a quick course in grammar and as a reference handbook. Keep the book on your desk or wherever you do most of your writing. If you use the text primarily as a reference handbook, simply reach for it whenever you have a question.

Here is how you can use the book for a quick course in practical grammar. If you commit yourself to improvement and devote your free time over a few days to the project, you will see quick progress in your grammatical skills. Allow yourself a week. Set aside the first two sessions (you'll need about two hours per sitting) to zero in on your grammatical weaknesses. During your first session, read quickly through Chapters 1 through 3; in the second session, read Chapters 4 through 6. Take brief notes on the grammatical errors you are inclined to make. Do not labor over this part of the project or take too much time: This first stage is designed to give you a fast overview and to isolate the grammatical mistakes on which you need to concentrate. At this stage, don't worry about understanding the various grammatical rules perfectly—thorough comprehension comes next.

After two sessions, you should have a few pages of notes listing the grammatical errors that trap you. This list constitutes your course outline. If you're like most people, you'll find your list is shorter than you expected: people know most of a language's grammar intuitively (though they may not be able to recite the rules that govern correct usage) and tend to make mistakes in only a few consistent areas.

Spend your next three or four sessions on stage two. Divide your course outline into three or four equal sections, and spend a few hours on each. In this second stage, thorough comprehension is your goal, and you should attain it by concentrating on each of your grammatical weaknesses in turn. Follow these steps for each grammatical error you have on your list:

Study the rule carefully. Absorb the logic of the rule; try to grasp its commonsense basis. Ask yourself *why* this rule exists—how does it ensure clarity? Don't waste time trying to memorize the rule. You'll forget memorized material very rapidly, but you'll retain material you genuinely absorb and understand. *Think* about the rule.

In your own words, write the rule out a few times, along with your brief explanation of the reason for the rule's existence. This procedure will help you absorb the rule more thoroughly and fix it more permanently in your mind.

Now turn to the example sentences for each rule. Study the incorrect examples first. Linger over them. Focus on each error, and understand fully *why* it's an error.

Next is the most important part of the procedure: turn to the correct examples, study them carefully, and compare them to the incorrect examples. Make sure you understand what's different about the correct examples—focus on the internal logic of the correct sentence, and on the way it fulfills the rule you studied in Steps 1 and 2. The key to success here, too, is grasping the commonsense reason that makes this form correct. *Think* about the correct sentence.

Finally, write out the correct example a few times, and follow it with correct examples of your own. You can check the structure of your sentences by comparing them to those in the book.

Having followed these steps, you can review and test your under-standing by taking the quiz at the end of each chapter. The quizzes focus on the errors people are most likely to make; these may or may not be the ones that cause problems for you. If you have understood the rules and examples, almost all or most of your answers will be correct. Answers and explanations follow each quiz to provide one more opportunity for you to understand the principles of grammar and usage involved in the questions.

Keep this book in a handy spot to use as a reference handbook and to jog your memory.

Good luck—and good writing!

Elaine Bender

I
INTRODUCTION TO GRAMMAR

The conventional classification of parts of speech is by form: noun, pronoun, verb, adjective, adverb, preposition, conjunction. The functional classification, which we use later in this book, groups parts of speech by use: subject, verb, complement, modifier, connective. In this section we define and illustrate these terms.

Parts of Speech—Classification by Form

Noun

A noun is a word used to name a person, place, thing, or quality.

Helen, Colorado, desk, truth

Pronoun

A pronoun is a word used in place of a noun. Pronouns are classified as:

PERSONAL:	I, we, you, she, him, it
RELATIVE:	who, which, that
INTERROGATIVE:	who, which, what
DEMONSTRATIVE:	this, that, these, those
INDEFINITE:	one, any, each, somebody
INTENSIVE AND REFLEXIVE:	myself, yourself, himself

Verb

A verb is a word or group of words that expresses being of the subject or action to or by the subject. The verb, together with any words that complete or modify its meaning, forms the predicate of the sentence.

am, is, walk, run, play

Adjective

An adjective is a word that describes or limits (modifies) the meaning of a noun or pronoun.

higher morale, *gray* stone, *rapid* growth

Adverb

An adverb is a word that modifies a verb, an adjective, or another adverb. It answers the questions where, when, how, or how much.

write *legibly*, long *enough*, *very* high production

Preposition

A preposition is a word used to relate a noun or pronoun to some other word in the sentence.

at, in, by, from, toward

Conjunction

A conjunction is a word used to join words, phrases, or clauses.

and, but, nor

Clause

A clause is a group of related words containing a subject and a predicate.

An *independent* (or main) clause makes a complete statement and is not introduced by any subordinating word. When it stands alone, it is a simple sentence.

We shall distribute the book by the end of the month.

A *dependent* (or subordinate) clause cannot stand alone as a complete sentence. It depends upon some words in the independent clause to complete its meaning. Dependent clauses are classified by function as:

ADJECTIVE: This is the customer *who wrote to us for information.*

I have the report *he is looking for.* ("that" is under stood)

ADVERB: *As soon as you have finished the memo,* bring it to my office.

NOUN: *Whoever conducts the meeting* will be able to answer your questions.

Can you tell me *what the meeting will be about?*

Phrase

A phrase is a group of related words without a subject or predicate used as a noun, adjective, adverb, or verb. Phrases are classified:

PREPOSITIONAL: Put the finished letter *on my desk.* (used as a noun)

PARTICIPIAL: The representative *giving the speech* works in my office. (used as an adjective)

GERUND: *Writing this report* has been a long and difficult job. (used as a noun)

INFINITIVE: Our purpose is *to make the instructions as useful as possible.* (used as a noun)

Sentence Classification

To construct sentences which will effectively convey your meaning to your readers, you must be able to recognize sentence classification and to know what kind of sentence does each writing job best. There are four types of sentences:

Simple Sentence

A simple sentence contains only one clause (an independent clause). This does not mean, however, that it must be short. It may include many phrases, a compound subject or predicate, and a number of modifiers.

> The book was returned.

> You should set forth your proposal in writing and enclose the latest balance sheets of the corporation.

Compound Sentence

A compound sentence has two or more independent clauses. Each of these clauses could be written as a simple sentence. There are no dependent clauses in a compound sentence.

> You may discuss this problem with your teacher, or you may speak to the principal.

Complex Sentence

A complex sentence contains one independent clause and one or more dependent clauses.

> When we were reviewing the attendance reports for February and March, we noted a number of inconsistencies.

Compound-Complex Sentence

A compound-complex sentence contains at least two independent clauses and one or more dependent clauses.

> Since that letter appears to answer your needs, we are enclosing a copy; we hope that it will answer all your questions fully.

Functional Classification of Sentence Parts

The parts of speech defined in this book are basic to a study of grammar. We can also group these parts according to their *use* and classify them by function as we use them elsewhere in the book.

The basic parts of the sentence are the subject, verb, and complement. Modifiers and connectives support this basic sentence, modifiers by making the meaning more exact and connectives by showing the relationship between parts.

Subject

The subject of a sentence is the word or group of words which names the thing, person, place, or idea about which the sentence makes a statement. The single words most often used as subjects are *nouns* and *pronouns.*

The *conductor* called the rehearsal for 3 o'clock. (noun)

He wants everybody to attend. (personal pronoun)

Two verbals—the *gerund* and, less often, the *infinitive*—may also be the subject of a sentence.

Walking is good exercise. (gerund)

To run is more tiring than to walk. (infinitive)

The *demonstrative, interrogative,* and *indefinite pronouns* are among the other parts of speech used as subjects.

That is going to be a difficult task. (demonstrative)

What are your plans for doing it? (interrogative)

Everyone is eager to have you succeed. (indefinite)

A *phrase* serving as a noun may be the subject of a sentence.

Studying carefully was the smartest thing the student did.

To make this report as comprehensive as possible is our objective.

An entire *dependent clause* may be used as the subject.

Whoever answers the telephone will be able to give you the information.

Whether the report has been released or not will determine our action.

In the chapters that follow you may find these five elements referred to generally as "substantives." A substantive is a noun or a word or group of words used as a noun.

Verb

The verb tells what the subject itself does (active verb), what something else does to the subject (passive verb), or what the subject is (linking verb). Every sentence must contain a verb. Verbals, although they come from verbs, cannot serve as verbs in the predicate of a sentence.

The properties of a verb are *number, person, tense, mood,* and *voice.* To indicate these properties we either change the form of the verb itself or add, to the main verb, other verb forms called *auxiliary verbs—be, have, can, may, might, shall, will, should, would, could, must, do.*

Number tells whether the verb is singular or plural; *person* tells whether the first person (*I*), second person (*you*), or third person (*he, it, they*) is performing the action. A verb and its subject must agree in number and person. This problem of agreement is covered in Chapter 3.

Tense is the means by which we show the time of an action— whether it happened in the past, is happening in the present, or will happen in the future. *Mood* (indicative, imperative, subjunctive) indicates the manner of assertion—statement, command, wish, or condition.

Voice is the property of a verb that indicates whether the object is performing or receiving the action of the verb. A verb in the *active voice* tells what the subject is doing; a verb in the *passive voice* tells what is being done to the subject.

> The technician *completed* the report on time. (The verb *completed,* in the active voice, tells what the subject, *technician,* did.)

> The report *was completed* on time. (The verb *was completed,* in the passive voice, tells what was done to the subject, *report.*)

Complement

The complement is the word or group of words that comes after the verb and completes its meaning. A complement may be (1) a direct object of the verb, (2) an indirect object of the verb, (3) a predicate nominative, or (4) a predicate adjective.

(1) *Direct object:*

> She gave the *report* to her secretary. (*Report* is the direct object of the verb.)
> We are trying *to find a solution to this problem.* (The infinitive phrase is the direct object of the verb.)
> Give me *whatever information you have.* (The noun clause is the direct object of the verb.)

(2) *Indirect object:*

> She gave (to) *her* the report. (*Her* is the indirect object of the verb; *report* is the direct object.)
> Give (to) *whoever answers the door* this letter. (The noun clause is the indirect object of the verb.)

(3) *Predicate nominative:*

> The predicate nominative is also called the *predicate noun, predicate complement,* or *subjective complement.* The predicate nominative follows a linking verb and renames the subject. It may be a noun, a pronoun, a verbal, a phrase, or a clause.

NOUN:	She is *chair* of the committee
PRONOUN:	They thought the author was *he.*
GERUND:	My favorite exercise is *swimming.*
INFINITIVE PHRASE:	The purpose of this memorandum is *to clarify the matter.*
NOUN CLAUSE:	The conference leader should be *whoever is best qualified.*

(4) *Predicate adjective:*

> A predicate adjective is an adjective (or adjective phrase) appearing in the predicate and modifying the subject. A predicate adjective occurs only after linking verbs and sense verbs.
>
> The flower smells *sweet.*
> The meeting we are planning for Tuesday will be *on that subject.*
> This material is *over my head.*

Modifiers

Modifiers—single words, phrases, or clauses—are used to limit, describe, or define some element of the sentence. They must be attached to a sentence element which is both clear and expressed. A modifier is said to dangle when it is not attached both logically and grammatically to a definite element in the sentence.

(1) *Adjectives* describe or limit the meaning of nouns or pronouns.

> The new employee has been assigned the difficult task of analyzing the *statistical* reports on import quotas.
>
> The report *of the financial committee* revealed a problem. (prepositional phrase used as an adjective)
>
> The report *submitted by the financial committee* revealed a problem. (participial phrase used as an adjective)

(2) *Adverbs* modify verbs, verbals, adjectives, or other adverbs. They answer the questions *where, how or how much, when, why.*

> We will hold the meeting *here.*
>
> She writes *fluently.*
>
> The meeting is scheduled *for 3 o'clock.*
>
> Bring me the letter *as soon as it is finished.*

Connectives

Connectives join one part of a sentence with another and show the relationship between the parts they connect. Conjunctions and prepositions are the most important connectives.

(1) Connectives joining elements of equal rank:

Coordinate conjunctions are perhaps the most used, and the most overused, connectives. They join sentence elements of equal grammatical importance—words with words, phrases with phrases, independent clauses with independent clauses. The coordinate conjunctions are:

and, but, or, nor, for, yet, so

Correlative conjunctions work in pairs to connect sentence elements of equal rank. Each member of a pair of correlative conjunctions must be followed by the same part of speech. Examples of these conjunctions are:

either ... or, neither ... nor, not only ... but also, both ... and

Conjunctive adverbs connect independent clauses and show a relation between them. Although the clause introduced by the conjunctive adverb is grammatically independent, it is logically dependent upon the preceding clause for its *complete* meaning. These are some conjunctive adverbs:

therefore, however, consequently, furthermore, moreover, nevertheless

(2) Connectives joining elements of unequal rank:

Subordinate conjunctions introduce dependent adverb clauses and join them to independent clauses. Some of these conjunctions are:

before, since, after, as, because, if, unless, until, although

Relative pronouns not only introduce noun and adjective clauses but also act as pronouns within their own clauses. These pronouns include:

that, which, who, whom, whatever, whichever, whoever

The client *who called for an appointment* has just arrived. (adjective clause)

When he calls, tell him *that I had to leave for a meeting.* (noun clause)

Relative adverbs introduce subordinate clauses. The most common of these connectives are:

how, where, when, while

(3) Prepositions:

A *preposition* connects its object with the word in the main clause that the prepositional phrase modifies; it shows the relationship between that word and the object of the preposition. Some prepositions are:

to, of, by, from, between, in, over, under, for

Verbals

Verbals are words formed from verbs; however, they can never act as verbs. They may serve as subject, complement, and modifier. The three kinds of verbals are gerunds, participles, and infinitives.

Infinitive (may or may not be preceded by *to*):

To screen these applications will take a long time. (subject)

Can you suggest someone *to speak* at the meeting? (complement)

I will be happy *to send you* the copy. (modifier)

Participle:

The outline, *covering* the main points of the discussion, has been prepared.

The main points of the discussion, *covered* by the outline, are these.

Having covered the main points of the discussion, the speaker ended his talk.

Gerund (the *-ing* form of the verb used as a noun):

Creating machinery to put the law into effect was an enormous task.

We will appreciate your *furnishing* this information.

Quiz

Because the terms and concepts in this chapter will be used throughout this book, you need to be sure you understand them. Taking the quiz below and reading the explanatory answers will help you to remember some key terms.

Directions: Underlined words and phrases in the paragraph below are preceded by a number. The list of terms is lettered. In your notes for this chapter, write the letter which names the underlined word or phrase next to the number.

(1) *Advertisements* appeal to consumers' needs and desires. They use (2) *subtle* methods (3) *to attract* us. Not only the language but also the images affect (4) *emotions*. Color is a (5) *contributor* to our reactions. Red may give (6) *to us* feelings of strong passions. Green, (7) *which* is nature's color, is (8) *peaceful*. (9) *Analyzing* advertisements (10) *carefully* (11) *reveals* their intentions.

A. Subject

B. Verb

C. Complement — direct object

D. Complement — indirect object

E. Complement — predicate nominative

F. Complement — predicate adjective

G. Modifier — adjective

H. Modifier — adverb

I. Relative pronoun

J. Verbal — infinitive

K. Verbal — gerund

Answers and Explanations

1–A. The noun *advertisements* names what the sentence will make a statement about.

2–G. *Subtle* describes the methods, and since it describes a noun, it is an adjective.

3–J. A verb preceded by *to* is an infinitive.

4–C. *Emotions* tells what is affected, so it is the direct object of that verb.

5–E. *Contributor* follows the linking verb *is* and renames the subject; therefore it is a predicate nominative.

6–D. *To us* completes the verb *give* by telling to whom feelings are given.

7–I. Relative pronouns act as the subject of their own clauses. Here, *which* refers to *green*, the subject of the main clause.

8–F. *Peaceful* describes *green*, the subject, and it is connected to the subject by a linking verb.

9–K. The *-ing* form of the verb analyze is used as a noun.

10–H. *Carefully* modifies the verb by describing when something is revealed.

11–B. *Reveals* expresses what *analyzing advertisements* does, so it is the verb.

2

NAMING WORDS—CASE AND GENDER

Naming Words

Nouns are the principal "naming" words; certain kinds of pronouns also name things and persons. Both nouns and pronouns serve as *subject* and as *complements*. If you are going to use them effectively, you should refresh your knowledge of the kinds or classes of nouns and pronouns and of the peculiar characteristics that may cause them to be troublesome. Let us consider, first, the characteristics (the grammatical properties) that nouns and pronouns have in common.

Characteristics of Nouns and Pronouns

Both nouns and pronouns have three properties: case, gender, and number.

Case is the property of a noun or pronoun which shows, either by inflection (change in the form of the noun or pronoun) or by position, the relation of the noun or pronoun to other parts of the sentence. English has three cases: nominative, objective, and possessive. This chapter gives and illustrates principles that you can follow to ensure the use of the appropriate case.

Gender states the sex of the object being named. In English, there are three grammatical genders: masculine, feminine, and neuter. To avoid sexism and stereotyping, the masculine pronoun should not be used to refer generically to persons of either sex. Gender neutral terms are also used rather than nouns which specify a role or profession. Examples of these usages occur at the end of this chapter.

Number is the property by which we indicate whether one thing or more than one is being named. In English, we recognize two numbers: singular and plural. You will encounter two problems in connection with the number of nouns and pronouns. The first is how to change a singular noun to a proper plural form. The second is how to accurately determine the number of the noun that is serving as a subject (or of the pronoun, which may depend on its antecedent for its number) so that you can make the verb agree with its subject in number. Agreement is discussed in Chapter 3.

Recognizing Nouns

Nouns are the principal naming words. To use them effectively, the writer needs background information about (1) the kinds or classes of nouns and (2) the grammatical properties of nouns. A noun names a person, thing, idea, place, or quality. There are five classes of nouns: proper, common, collective, concrete, and abstract.

A *proper* noun names a particular place, person, or thing. The chief problem with proper nouns is recognizing them so that you can capitalize them.

Atlanta, Mrs. Reese, Prime Minister Blair

A *common* noun in the singular names a class or group of persons, places, or things.

Teacher, state, automobile

A *collective* noun, singular in form, names a group or collection of individuals. The chief problem with collective nouns is determining the number of the verb to use with the collective noun. For this reason, it is discussed at length in the next chapter under agreement of subject and verb.

committee, jury, council, task force, class

A *concrete* noun names something that can be perceived by the senses.

Apple, pencil, computer

An *abstract* noun names a quality, state, or idea.

justice, objectivity, happiness

Recognizing Pronouns

Pronouns are the second type of naming words. They stand in place of nouns. The six classes of pronouns are: personal, relative, interrogative, indefinite, demonstrative, and intensive and reflexive.

The *personal* pronoun shows which person (first, second, or third) is the subject. Personal pronouns are troublesome because of their many forms; they change form to indicate number, person, and case.

FIRST PERSON: I, we, me, us, my, mine, our, ours

SECOND PERSON: you, your, yours

THIRD PERSON: he, she, it, they, his, hers, its, theirs, him, her, them, their

The *relative* pronoun serves two purposes: (1) it takes the place of a noun in the clause it introduces, and (2) like a conjunction, it connects its clause with the rest of the sentence.

who, whom, which, that, whoever, whomever, whichever, whatever

The relative pronoun, like the personal pronoun, changes form to indicate number, person, and case.

The *interrogative* pronouns have the same forms as relative pronouns, but differ in function. The interrogative pronoun asks a question.

who, whom, which, what

The *indefinite* pronouns listed here are singular, as are most indefinites.

another, anyone, each, either, everyone, no one, nothing

The *demonstrative* pronouns point out or refer to a substantive which has been clearly expressed or just as clearly implied. They may be used as pronouns

These are the toys he wants.

or as adjectives.

Bring me *those* toys.

Note: Do not use the personal pronoun *them* as an adjective. Use either of the demonstratives, *these* or *those,* instead.

NOT: Give *them* letters to the messenger.
BUT: Give *those* letters to the messenger.
OR: Give *them* to the messenger.

Both *intensive* and *reflexive* pronouns are compound personal pronouns:

myself, yourself, himself, herself, itself, ourselves, yourselves, themselves

Note: An intensive pronoun emphasizes or intensifies a meaning. It is not set off by commas.

I *myself* will see that it is done.

The teacher *himself* gave the order.

I will take it to her *myself.*

A reflexive pronoun appears as the direct object of a verb, and its antecedent serves as the subject of the verb.

I taught *myself* how to type.

She hurt *herself* when she fell.

It can, however, be the object of a preposition,

He finished the assignment by *himself*

She was beside *herself* with joy.

the indirect object of a verb,

I bought *myself* a new dress yesterday.

or a predicate nominative.

I am just not *myself* today.

The reflexive pronoun is not used where the shorter personal pronoun can be substituted for it with no change in meaning.

NOT: Both the Principal and *myself* endorse the policy.

BUT: Both the Principal and *I* endorse the policy.

Note: Most errors (usually in speech) in the use of these pronouns are such careless errors as:

The use of *hisself* for *himself.*

The use of *theirselves* for *themselves.*

The use of *myself* instead of the personal pronoun *me* or *I* in such constructions as "The attorney and *myself* were assigned to do this work."

Case

Case is the property of a noun or pronoun which shows, either by inflection (change in form) or by position, the relation of the word to other parts of the sentence. English has three cases: *nominative, objective,* and *possessive.*

All nouns and a few pronouns keep the same form in the nominative and in the objective cases. Thus, we must depend on the position of these words in the sentence to indicate their function. Since nouns don't change form to indicate nominative and objective case, our only real difficulty with them comes in the formation and use of the possessive.

On the other hand, some pronouns are inflected (change form) in the nominative and objective cases as well as in the possessive. Because of this, the case of pronouns causes us more trouble than does the case of nouns, and pronouns are more frequently misused.

Nominative Case

The nominative (or subjective) case is used primarily to name the subject of a verb or the predicate complement after a linking verb (such as *seem, appear,* or any form of *be*).

If either the subject or predicate complement is compound, both members must be in the nominative case.

NOT: Either *she* or *me* will be responsible.

BUT: Either *she* or *I* will be responsible. (Either *she* will be ... or *I* will be....)

Note: An appositive, which is a word or group of words standing next to another word and denoting the same person or thing, is always in the same case as its antecedent (the word it stands in apposition to). Therefore, *if the antecedent is in the nominative case,* the appositive must also be in the nominative case. If the antecedent is in the objective case, the appositive is also in the objective case.

NOT: The representatives, *Tonya and me,* are to meet on Friday.

BUT: The representatives, *Tonya and I,* are to meet on Friday. (*Tonya and I* are to meet...)

Subject of a Verb in a Main Clause

A noun or pronoun serving as the subject of a verb (except the subject of an infinitive) is in the nominative case.

I was late for work this morning. (*I* is in the nominative case.)

He is planning to finish his report this week.

She and I have been assigned a new project. (Both words joined by the coordinate conjunction are in the nominative case.)

The pronoun *who* used as the subject of a verb is not affected by a parenthetical expression such as *I think, he believes, they say* intervening between the subject and the verb.

He is the person *who* I think *is* best qualified. (Disregard "I think"; who is the subject of the clause.)

We asked Susan, *who* we knew *had always been* a student of English. (Ignore "we knew"; who is the subject of the clause.)

Mr. Chen is the attorney *who* we suppose *will prepare* the brief.

("We suppose" is a parenthetical expression; who is the subject of the clause.)

The interrogative pronouns (e.g., who, which, what) appear to require the nominative case because they usually come first in the sentence. In informal writing and speaking we may put these pronouns in the nominative case; in other types of writing the interrogative pronoun takes the case called for by its function in the sentence.

INFORMAL: *Who* did you send the information to?

FORMAL: *Whom* did you send the information to?
or: To *whom* did you send the information?

Subject of a Relative Clause

A relative pronoun (e.g., who, whoever, which, whichever) used as the subject of a clause is in the nominative case.

Send this e-mail to *whoever requested the information* about the product.

The clause itself may be a subject or, as in this example, an object; however, the case of the relative pronoun depends upon its use *within* the clause.

The awards will go to those *who complete* the course with the highest score. (The antecedent of the relative pronoun—those—is in the objective case, but *who* is in the nominative case because it is the subject of the clause.)

Whoever is selected must report on Monday. (The clause is the subject of the sentence; the relative pronoun is in the nominative case because it is the subject of the clause.)

Subject of a Clause Introduced by *Than* or *As*

If the word following *than* or *as* introduces a clause (even if part of the clause is understood), that word must be in the nominative case. But if the word following *than* or *as* does not introduce a clause, it must be in the objective case. To test whether the word should be in the nominative or objective case, complete the clause.

> She has been here longer than *he*. (than *he has*)
>
> Leroy is a better student than *I*. (than *I am*)
>
> They were as late as *we* in filing the report. (as *we were*)
>
> We arrived as promptly as *they*. (as *they were*)

In the following examples, the word following *than* or *as* may be in either the nominative or the objective case, depending on the intended meaning. If there is any chance your meaning might be misunderstood, complete the clause.

> She likes this work better than I. (than *I like it*)
> She likes this work better than *me*. (than *she likes me*)
> I have known Kim as long as *she*. (as *she has*)
> I have known Kim as long as *her*. (*as I have known her*)

Words Following Forms of *Be* (Predicate Nominative)

A noun or pronoun following a form of the verb *be* (except for the infinitive if it has its own subject) must be in the nominative case. (This word is called the *predicate nominative* or, if a noun, the *predicate noun*.) The general rule applying to this construction is that the word following the verb *be* must be in the same case as the word before the verb. Imagine that the verb *be* has the same meaning as the equals sign (=) in mathematics.

> NOT: They thought I was *him*.
> BUT: They thought I was *he*. ($I = he$)

> NOT: I am expecting my accountant to call. Is that *her*?
> BUT: I am expecting my accountant to call. Is that *she*?

A noun or pronoun following the infinitive *to be* is in the nominative case if the infinitive has no subject.

> He was thought to be *I*.
>
> My brother was taken to be *I*.

Note: People frequently have trouble when one or both of the members of the compound subject or predicate nominative are pronouns. Try this simple test: Decide which case would be appropriate if *one* pronoun were the simple subject or predicate nominative, and then use the same case for both.

Example: The new *representatives* are *he and I.*
Reverse positions: *He and I* are the new *representatives.*

Example: If any one of the members is chosen, *it* should be *he.*
Reverse positions: If any one of the members is chosen, *he* should be *it.*

Example: The *author* was thought to be *I.*
Reverse positions: *I* was thought to be the *author.*

Direct Address

Direct address is a construction used parenthetically to direct a speech to some particular person. Nouns or pronouns in direct address are in the nominative case and are set off by commas. This construction will cause little trouble since proper names, which are the main examples of direct address, do not change form to indicate case.

James, come here for a minute.

It is true, *sir,* that I made that remark.

Tell me, *Doctor,* does the medication have side effects?

Nominative Absolute

The nominative absolute is a phrase that consists of a noun or a pronoun and a participle. It modifies the whole sentence but is grammatically independent of the rest of the sentence. The noun or pronoun in a nominative construction is in the nominative case.

We left the office together, *he having finished his work.* (The phrase beginning *he having finished* is a nominative absolute phrase modifying the main clause. The pronoun *he is* the subject of the *action implied* by the participle *having finished;* it is in the nominative case.)

She having been elected foreperson, I am sure the jury deliberations will be orderly.

Objective Case

The objective (or accusative) case is used chiefly to name the receiver or object of the action of a verb or to name the object of a preposition.

When one part of a compound expression (joined by a coordinate conjunction) is in the objective case, all other parts of the same expression must also be in the objective case.

When you reach the station call either *him* or *me.* (*call him …* or *call me*)

The work was given to *you* and *me.* (*to you … to me*)

When the antecedent of an appositive is in the objective case because it is serving a function that requires that case, the appositive must also be in the objective case.

The boss has appointed *us, you and me,* to the committee. (*has appointed you … has appointed me*)

She gave *us teachers a* copy of the report. (*she gave us …*) That principle is basic to *us Americans.* (*is basic to us*)

Direct Object of a Verb or Verbal

A noun or pronoun serving as the direct object of a verb or verbal is in the objective case.

The contractor telephoned *him* at his office. *(Him* is the object of the verb *telephoned.*)

My supervisor called *her* and *me* to the office. (The compound object *her and me* is the object of the verb *called.*)

They will invite *us technicians* to the meeting. (*Us*, as well as its appositive *technicians*, is the object of the verb *invite*.)

Having called *him* and told *him* of our plan, we left the house. (The first *him* is the direct object of the participle *having called;* the second *him* is the object of the participle *having told*.)

Indirect Object of a Verb or Verbal

A word used as the indirect object of a verb or verbal is in the objective case.

The engineer gave *me* the manual. (*Me* is the indirect object of the verb *gave*.)

The representative showed *us users* how to access the new program. (*Us*, as well as its appositive *users*, is the indirect object of the verb *showed*.)

A letter giving *him* authority to represent the company is being prepared. (*Him* is the indirect object of the participle *giving*.)

Object of a Preposition

A noun or pronoun serving as the object of a preposition is in the objective case.

Be sure to give the report to *him*. (*Him* is the object of the preposition *to*.)

Several of *us* are concerned about the situation. (*Us* is the object of the preposition *of*.)

He assigned the task of reviewing the report to *him* and *me*. (*Him and me* is the compound object of the preposition *to*.)

Whom did you give the fax to? (The interrogative pronoun *whom* is the object of the preposition *to*.)

The person to *whom* this fax is addressed has left the office. (The relative pronoun *whom* is the object of the preposition *to* in the relative clause.)

But: Give this fax to *whoever* is available to reply to it. (Although the clause *whoever is available* is the object of the preposition *to,* the relative pronoun *whoever* is in the nominative case because it is the subject of its own clause.)

Note: But is a preposition when *except* may be substituted for it with no change in meaning.

Everyone is going *but* me. (Everyone is going *except* me.)

A special troublemaker is the compound object *you and me* after the preposition *between.* Do not write *between you and I;* write *between you and me.*

NOT: The plan divides operations between *you and I.*
BUT: The plan divides operations between *you and me.*

Subject of an Infinitive

A noun or pronoun used as the subject of an infinitive is in the objective case.

I want *him* to have this copy. (*Him* is the subject of the infinitive *to have.*)

We expect *her* to be elected. (*Her* is the subject of the infinitive *to be elected.*)

They invited *him and me* to attend the reception. (*Him and me* is the compound subject of the infinitive *to attend.*)

Whom do they expect to be the next delegate to the convention? (*Whom* is the subject of the infinitive *to be.*)

Word Following Infinitive *To Be*

Previously we saw that the verb *to be* takes the same case after it as before it. Since the subject of an infinitive is in the objective case, a word following the infinitive is also in the objective case.

I believe *him* to be honest. (*Him* is the subject of *to be.*)

They thought him to be *me*. (Reverse to test choice of case: They thought *me* to be *him*.)

We assumed the author of the letter to be *her*. (Reverse: We assumed *her* to be the *author* ...)

Subject of a Participle

The subject of a participle is in the objective case. The writer's problem comes in determining whether a verbal is a participle or a gerund. Both may have the same form (the *-ing* form of the verb), but only the subject of the *participle* is in the objective case. The choice depends on your meaning. This technique may help you choose the correct case: When the *doer* of the action is stressed, the verbal is a participle performing its adjective function as a modifier of its subject; when the *action itself* is the important thing, the verbal is a gerund—a verbal noun.

Imagine *him* flying an airplane. (The element being stressed here is the pronoun *him*; therefore, the verbal *flying* is a participle modifying *him*, and the pronoun *him* is in the objective case.)

Imagine his *flying* to Paris. (Here we are stressing not *him* but his *flying*; therefore, the verbal *flying* is a gerund, and the pronoun *his* is in the possessive case.)

NOT: I appreciate *him* tutoring me.
BUT: I appreciate *his* tutoring me.

What is appreciated is the *tutoring*; therefore, the verbal tutoring is a gerund, and the pronoun is possessive.

Possessive Case

The possessive case is used to indicate ownership.

Possessive of Singular Words

To form the possessive of singular words not ending in -*s* (including the indefinite pronouns), add the apostrophe and -*s*.

> the *teacher's* report; the *President's* office; the *secretary's* desk; *anyone's* guess; *somebody's* coat

Note: When *else* is used with an indefinite pronoun, form the possessive by adding the apostrophe and -*s* to *else*, rather than to the indefinite pronoun.

> *somebody's* coat   but: somebody *else's* coat
> *anyone's* idea   but: anyone *else's* idea

To form the possessive of a singular common noun ending in -*s* or an *s*-sound, add the apostrophe and -*s*.

Singular form	*Possessive form*
boss	boss's (pronounced boss-es)
class	class's (prounounced class-es)
axe	axe's (pronounced axe-es)

To form the possessive of a proper noun ending in -*s* or an *s* sound, add apostrophe and *s*, unless awkward pronunciation results. If this is the case, using the apostrophe only is acceptable. Since determining whether pronunciation is awkward is a subjective judgment, either form is acceptable.

> Charles's accounts
> Lois's files
> Sophocles's or Sophocles' plays

The apostrophe is omitted in some organization or geographical names that contain a possessive thought. Follow the form used by the organization itself.

> Harpers Ferry   Pikes Peak
>
> Governors Island   Citizens National Bank

Do not use the apostrophe in forming the possessive of the personal and relative pronouns. The possessive forms of these pronouns are:

RELATIVE: whose

PERSONAL: her, hers (not her's), his, their, theirs, our, ours, my, mine, your, yours, its

Note: Its is the possessive form of the personal pronoun *it*; *it's* is a contraction of *it is*. Similarly, *whose* is the possessive form of the relative pronoun *who*, and *who's* is a contraction of *who is*. The examples below illustrate the correct use of these words.

Its operation is simple.

It's (it is) simple to operate.

Whose coat is that?

Who's (who is) going with me?

Possessive of Plural Words

To form the possessive of a plural word not ending in -*s*, add the apostrophe and -*s*.

men's, children's, women's, people's

To form the possessive of a plural word ending in -*s*, add the apostrophe only.

All of the teachers' reports have been received.

Use the *of* phrase to form the possessive of names consisting of several words, in order to avoid an awkward construction.

NOT: The local chapter of the National Association of Radio and Television Broadcasters' first meeting was held Thursday.

BUT: The first meeting of the local chapter of the National Association of Radio and Television Broadcasters was held Thursday.

Sometimes either the *of* phrase or the possessive is needed to avoid ambiguity.

NOT: This is the *President's picture*. (Could mean: This is a portrait of him. OR: This is his property.)
BUT: This is *a picture of the President*. (his portrait)
OR: This is *a picture of the President's*. (his property)

Use the *of* phrase to avoid adding a possessive to a pronoun that is already possessive.

NOT: We are going to a *friend of mine's house*.
BUT: We are going to the *house of a friend of mine*.

Possessive of Compound Words

Form the possessive on the last word of a compound word, whether or not the compound is hyphenated. A point to remember is that, even though the plural of a compound word is formed by adding -*s* to the principal noun in the compound, the possessive is always formed by adding the *sign of the possessive* to the *last word in the compound*.

Singular possessive	*Plural*	*Plural possessive*
notary public's	notaries public	notaries public's
supervisor in charge's	supervisors in charge	supervisors in charge's
mother-in-law's	mothers-in-law	mothers-in-law's

If a possessive is followed by an appositive or an explanatory phrase, form the possessive on the explanatory word.

That was *Mrs. Kline your teacher's* idea.

I was acting on *my attorney Mr. Brown's* advice.

Have you read *the Senator from Arizona's* speech?

Note: The methods just illustrated are grammatically correct ways to show possession; they do, however, sound awkward. To make your writing more effective (and just as correct), try using an *of* phrase to form the possessive of compound words.

NOT: That was Ms. Kline your teacher's advice.
BUT: That was the advice of Ms. Kline, your teacher.

NOT: I was acting on my attorney Mr. Brown's advice.
BUT: I was acting on the advice of my attorney, Mr. Brown.

Joint, Separate, and Alternative Possession

When two or more people possess the same thing jointly, form the possessive on the last word only.

She is *Mr. Roberts and Ms. Henry's* coach. (She is coach to both people.)

These pictures are from *Bill and Hillary's* vacation trip.

Note: When one of the words involved in the joint possession is a pronoun, each word must be in the possessive.

This is *Roberto's, Josie's, and my* office.

Have you seen *Kobe's and his* new home?

When it is intended that each of the words in a series possess something individually, form the possessive on each word.

Paul's and Lee's handwriting are certainly different.

The *Deans' and the Professors'* associations are meeting here this week.

When alternative possession is intended, each word must be in the possessive.

I wouldn't want either *George's or Harry's* job.

Is that the *author's or the editor's* opinion?

Possessive of Abbreviations

Possessives of abbreviations are formed in the same way as are other possessives. Ordinarily the possessive sign is placed after the final period of the abbreviation.

Singular possessive	*Plural*	*Plural possessive*
M.D.'s	M.D.s	M.D.s'
Dr.'s	Drs.	Drs.'
Co.'s	Cos.	Cos.'
Bro.'s	Bros.	Bros.'

Enclosed is Johnson *Bros.'* bill for their work.

John Blank, *Jr.'s* account has been closed.

Parallel Possessives

Be sure that a word standing parallel with a possessive is itself possessive in form.

NOT: *Her* work, like an *accountant,* is exacting.
BUT: *Her* work, like an *accountant's,* is exacting.

NOT: *His* task is no more difficult than his *neighbor.*
BUT: *His* task is no more difficult than his *neighbor's.*

Possessive with a Gerund

A noun or pronoun immediately preceding a gerund (a verbal noun naming an action) is in the possessive case. A participle, which may have the same form as a gerund, functions as an adjective; its subject is in the objective case.

Our being late delayed the meeting.

Terry's being late delayed the meeting.

You can always depend on *his* doing a good job.

Jim's writing the letter made all the difference.

Note: There are three exceptions to this general rule:

(1) The possessive of an inanimate object is not usually formed by the apostrophe and *-s*. When the subject of a gerund is a noun standing for an inanimate object, use the objective case, an *of* phrase, or a subordinate clause, whichever is most appropriate.

NOT: The *desk's refinishing* is almost complete.
BUT: The *refinishing of the desk* is almost complete. *(of* phrase)

NOT: The possibility of the *meeting's ending* soon is doubtful.
BUT: The possibility of the *meeting ending* soon is doubtful. (objective case)

NOT: We missed our ride because of the *meeting's lasting so late.*
BUT: We missed our ride because the *meeting lasted so late.* (subordinate clause)

(2) Do not use the possessive case for the subject of a gerund unless the subject immediately precedes the gerund. If subject and gerund are separated by other words, the subject must be in the objective case.

NOT: I can see no reason for a *student's* with his background *failing* to pass the test.
BUT: I can see no reason for a *student* with his background *failing* to pass the test. (Without intervening words: I can see no reason for a *student's failing* to pass the test.)

NOT: I concede the difficulty of *his,* because of his interest, *being* completely fair.
BUT: I concede the difficulty of *him,* because of his interest, *being* completely fair.

(3) There are no possessive forms for the demonstrative pronouns *that, this, these,* and *those.* Therefore, when these words are used as subjects of a gerund they do not change form.

NOT: We cannot be sure of *that's* being true.
BUT: We cannot be sure of *that* being true.

NOT: What are the chances of *this'* being sold?
BUT: What are the chances of *this* being sold?

Gender

Avoiding Sexist Language

Do not use the pronouns *he*, *him*, and *his* to refer generically to persons of either sex. Although *he/she*, *him/her* and *his/hers* are acceptable usage, these phrases produce awkward sentences. A better strategy makes the antecedent of the pronoun plural, or replaces the pronoun with a noun phrase.

NOT: Every employee has his own cell phone
BUT: All employees have their own cell phones.
OR: Every employee has a personal cell phone.

Nouns that describe roles or professions which can be performed by either sex should also be gender neutral. Instead of *chairman* or *chairwoman*, use *chair* or *head*.

NOT	BUT
congressman	representative
fireman	firefighter
forefathers	ancestors
mailman	letter carrier
manpower	personnel
mankind	humanity, people
policeman	police officer
salesman, saleslady	sales clerk, sales associate, sales representative
waiter, waitress	server

Quiz

To review your knowledge of the usages explained in this chapter, take the following quiz.

Directions: Read the following sentences for problems involving the use of naming words. If you find an error, rewrite the sentence. If the sentence is correct, write "correct."

1. I scheduled a meeting between the client and myself.

2. The accountants, Tanika and me, audited the quarterly statements.

3. Riley, whom I know has word processing skills, will edit the document.

4. Whom did the President send to represent our nation at the treaty conference?

5. Ali arrived as quickly as we.

6. When you receive the survey responses, inform him or I of the results.

7. The updated financial report will be sent to her and me.

8. Data processing duties will be divided between you and I.

9. The cell phone's battery is low.

10. Texas's flag features a single star.

11. The screen saver is the same on your's and my computer.

12. Its obvious that someone made an error.

Answers and Explanations

1. I scheduled a meeting between the client and *me.* The reflexive pronoun is not used where the shorter personal pronoun can be substituted for it.

2. The accountants, Tanika and *I,* audited the quarterly state-

ments. The appositive is in the same case as its antecedent. Since *accountants* is in the nominative case, the pronoun also must be nominative.

3. Riley, *who* I know has word processing skills, will edit the document. The pronoun *who* used as the subject of a verb is not affected by a parenthetical expression. *Who* is the subject of *has word processing skills.*

4. Correct. *Whom* did the President sent to represent our nation at the treaty conference? The context indicates a formal situation. Therefore, the interrogative pronoun, which in this sentence is the complement of the verb *send*, should be *whom.*

5. Correct. Ali arrived as quickly as *we.* If the word *as* introduces a clause, even if the clause is not stated completely, it must be in the nominative case. Here, the clause would be *as quickly as we did.*

6. When you receive the survey responses, inform him or *me* of the results. When one part of a compound expression is in the objective case, the other part or parts of the same expression must be in the objective case. The pronouns are the object of the verb *inform.*

7. Correct. The updated financial report will be sent to *her* and *me.* The same rule applies as in item 6. Here, the pronouns are the object of the preposition *to.*

8. Correct. Data processing duties will be divided between you and *me. Between* is a preposition, so pronouns following it must be in the objective case.

9. Correct. The cell phone's battery is low. Form the plural of nouns that do not end in *s* by adding apostrophe and *s.*

10. Correct. *Texas's* flag features a single star. Form the plural or proper nouns ending in *s* by adding *'s.*

11. The screen saver is the same on *your* and my computers. The possessive pronouns do not contain an apostrophe.

12. *It's* obvious that someone made an error. *Its* is a possessive pronoun. *It's* is a contraction of the phrase *it is.*

3
AGREEMENT AND REFERENCE

Agreement is the logical relationship between parts of speech in a sentence. There can be no good, clear sentences without agreement. Grammar starts here. The parts of the sentence must be in harmony with one another (must *agree*) if they are to express a clear thought.

Agreement of subject and verb is the heart of the good sentence. A sentence is simply a union of a *thing* (the subject) and an *action* (the verb). These two must agree; in fact, their agreement creates the sentence.

Other parts of the sentence, of course, must also be in agreement. Perhaps next in importance to the agreement of subject and verb is the agreement of a pronoun with its antecedent. It is these two areas that we will discuss in this chapter since there is a relationship between the principles governing each.

Agreement of Subject and Verb

The verb must agree with the subject in number and in person. If the subject is singular, the verb form must also be singular; if the subject is in the third person—*it, they*—the verb must also be in the third person.

The pronoun must agree with its antecedent (the word to which it refers—sometimes called its "referent") in number, in person, and in gender. Of the three, gender causes the least difficulty. However, as Chapter 2 explains, gender choices should avoid sexist language. The chief problem is identifying the antecedent and determining its number, person, and gender.

Agreement of Both Verb and Pronoun with Subject-Antecedent

Often the subject of the verb is also the antecedent of the pronoun. One might think that this would greatly simplify things. And to some extent it does; for once you have determined that the subject-antecedent is singular, you know where you stand—both verb and pronoun must likewise be singular. But be consistent; don't confuse your reader by shifting from a singular verb (which properly agrees with its singular subject) to a plural pronoun later in the sentence.

Subject Problems

The first step in making the parts of a sentence agree is to identify the subject. No one should have difficulty in identifying the routine subject of a sentence and in determining its number, person, and gender. In this section, therefore, we will discuss only those subjects that may present special problems.

Collective Words

A collective names a group of people or things. Although usually singular in form, it is treated as either singular or plural according to the sense of the sentence:

Singular when members of the group act, or are considered, as a *unit*:

The Promotion Committee *is visiting* the head office this week.

Plural when the members act, or are considered, *individually*:

The jury *are* unable to agree on a verdict.

The National Marketing Team *pool* the data *they* gather and *prepare their* report.

Common Collectives

assembly, association, audience, board, cabinet, class, commission, committee, company, corporation, council, counsel, couple, crowd, department, family, firm, group, jury, majority, minority, number, pair, press, public, staff, team, United States

Company Names as Collectives

Company names also qualify as collectives and may be either

singular or plural. Usually those ending with a singular sound are considered singular; those with a plural sound, plural.

> Flowers, Inc., *mails its* advertisements in envelopes with floral decorations.

> Jones Brothers *have sent their* representative to the conference.

A name ending in *Company* or *Corporation*, though usually considered singular, may—if the sense of the sentence requires—be used as a plural.

> The X Company *is* not on the list of approved organizations.

> The ABC Corporation *report* on the activities of *their* subsidiaries tomorrow morning.

Short Collectives

The following short words—though seldom listed as collectives—are governed by the rule for collectives. They are singular or plural according to the intended meaning of the sentence.

> all, any, more, most, none, some, who, which

When a prepositional phrase follows the word, the number of the noun in the phrase controls the number of the verb. When no such phrase follows, the writer signals his intended meaning by his choice of the singular or the plural verb.

> Some of the *work has been done.*
> Some of the *reports have been filed.*

> Most of the *correspondence is routine.*
> Most of the *rules are acceptable.*

> *Is* there *any* left? (any portion—any paper, any cake)
> *Are* there *any* left? (any individual items—any forms, any copies)

> *Which is* to be mailed? (which one)
> *Which are* to be mailed? (which ones)

Note: Many people treat none as singular in every instance, since it means *no one* or *not one*. This usage is correct. It is also acceptable, however, to treat *none* as plural when it is followed by a prepositional phrase which has a plural object. However, in formal English, the singular is preferred.

None of the applicants *is* eligible.

Units of Measure

When a number is used with a plural noun to indicate a unit of measurement (money, time, fractions, portions, distance, weight, quantity, etc.), a singular verb is used. When the term is thought of as individual parts, a plural verb is used.

Twenty dollars is the amount due.
Twenty dollars are in this stack.

Ten years seems like a long time.
Ten years have gone by since I last saw Paris.

Twenty-one pages is our goal for each writing session.
Twenty-one pages are needed to finish the job.

When fractions and expressions, such as *the rest of, the remainder of, a part of, percent of,* are followed by a prepositional phrase, the noun or pronoun in that phrase governs the number of the verb.

Four-fifths of the job was finished on time.
Four-fifths of the letters *were* finished on time.

The *rest* (or *remainder)* of the report *is* due Friday.
The *rest* (or *remainder)* of the letters *were* mailed today.

What *percent* of the information *is* available?
What *percent* of the items were lost?

Confusing Singular and Plural Forms

It is sometimes hard for us to tell by its forms whether a word is singular or plural. Some words that end in *-s* may be singular, and some seemingly singular words may be plural. These words are singular although they are plural in form: *apparatus, news, summons, whereabouts*.

The *news is* disturbing.

The thief's *whereabouts has* not yet been determined.

These words are plural, though they are singular (or collective) in meaning: *assets, earnings, odds, premises, proceeds, quarters, savings, wages, winnings.*

The company's *assets are* listed on the attached statement.

Earnings are up this quarter.

The *odds are* against our settling this case swiftly.

The *proceeds are* earmarked for her college education.

These words may be either singular or plural, depending on their meaning, even though they are plural in form: *ethics, goods, gross, headquarters, mechanics, politics, series, species, statistics, tactics.*

Ethics is a subject on which Josephson is well qualified to speak.
Watson's business *ethics are* above question.

Statistics is the only course I failed in school.
The *statistics prove* that I am right.

A gross of pencils *is* not enough.
A gross of pencils *are* being used.

A series of errors *has* marked our attempt.
A series of rain storms *are* needed to end the drought.

These nouns are plural, though they may appear to be singular because they have foreign or unusual plural form: *analyses, bases, phenomena, criteria.*

The analyses have been completed. *(Analyses* is the plural of *analysis.)*

What *are* your *bases* for these conclusions? *(Bases* is the plural of *basis.)*

Some interesting *phenomena are* disclosed in this report. *(Phenomena* is the plural of *phenomenon.)*

His conclusion seems sound, but his *criteria are* not valid. *(Criteria* is the plural of *criterion*.)

Note: Data, media, and *memoranda* require special mention. *Data* is the plural of *datum*; we must treat it as a plural when it refers to individual facts. But when *data* refers to a mass of facts as a unit, it more closely resembles a collective noun and may therefore be treated as a singular form.

The *data* from our last study *are* being analyzed.

This *data is* of the highest importance to our cause.

Media is the plural of *medium*. *Media* can be a collective used as a collective noun, either singular or plural. However, when used to refer to one means of mass communication, such as television or newspaper, the singular *media* should be used.

An advertising campaign to launch the new product appeared in the *media*.

Television was the preferred *medium* for the advertisements.

Memoranda is the Latin plural of *memorandum*; the English plural is *memorandums*. Either form is correct.

EITHER: These *memoranda* have been signed.

OR: These *memorandums* have been signed.

Indefinite Pronouns

These indefinite pronouns are singular. When they are used as subjects, they require singular verbs; when used as antecedents, they require singular pronouns:

anybody, anyone, any one (any one of a group), anything, each, either, every, everybody, everyone, every one (every one of a group), everything, neither, nobody, no one, nothing, one, somebody, someone, some one (some one of a group), something

Anyone is welcome, as long as *he* (not *they*) behaves himself.

Any one of the women *is* capable of doing it.

Each of us *is* required to sign *her* own name.

Either of the alternatives *is* suitable.

Everyone must buy his book for the course.

Every one of the employees *wishes* to sign the card.

Everything seems to be going smoothly now.

Neither of the plans *is* workable.

No one believes that our plan will work.

Someone has to finish this report.

Some one of you *has* to be responsible for it.

Even when two indefinite pronouns are joined by *and,* they remain singular in meaning.

Anyone and *everyone* is invited.

Nothing and *no one* escapes our attention.

When *each* or *every* is used to modify a compound subject (subjects joined by *and),* the subject is considered singular.

Every ball player and *sportscaster has joined* the club.

When *each* is inserted (as a parenthetic or explanatory element) between a plural or a compound subject and its plural verb, neither the plural form of the verb nor the plural form of the pronoun is affected.

The *leaders each want* the requirements changed.

The *students each have requested* permission to change *their* programs.

Many a (unlike *many*) is singular in meaning and takes a singular verb and pronoun.

Many a new employee feels insecure during *his* first few weeks on the job.

But: *Many employees feel* insecure during *their* first few weeks on the job.

More than one, though its meaning is plural, is used in the singular.

More than one vacation plan *was* changed because of the requirement.

More than one team *is* needed to handle the additional workload.

These words are plural: *both, few, many, several, others.*

Both of us *have received* new responsibilities.

Few will be able to finish their work on time.

Many plan to work all weekend.

Several of the teams *have submitted* their rosters, but *others* have not yet *finished theirs.*

Relative Pronouns

The verb in a relative clause must agree in number and in person with the antecedent of the relative pronoun (who, which, that) serving as the subject of the clause. Therefore, we must locate the antecedent and determine its person and number.

Have you talked with the customer *who was* waiting to see you? (*Customer* is the antecedent of the relative pronoun *who*, and the verb *was* must agree with this antecedent in person and number.)

Where are the books *that were* left on the table? (The verb in the relative clause—*were*—must agree with the relative pronoun—*that*—which must agree with its antecedent—*books*.)

We *who have* seen them practice predict their success. (The relative pronoun is *who*; the verb in the relative clause is *have*; the antecedent of the relative pronoun is *we*.)

In sentences that contain the phrases *one of the* or *one of those,* the antecedent of the relative pronoun is not *one* but the plural words that follow.

One of the letters *that were* on my desk has disappeared. (*One has disappeared,* or *One of the letters has disappeared,* is the main thought of the sentence. *That were on my desk* is a clause modifying *letters,* not *one;* thus the relative pronoun *that* must agree with *letters,* its antecedent, making the verb in the relative clause, *were,* plural.)

Here is one of those candidates *who are* applying for the position. (The antecedent of the relative pronoun *who* is the plural noun *candidates,* not the singular *one.*)

One of the representatives *who are* attending the meeting is wanted on the telephone. (The antecedent of the relative pronoun *who* is the plural noun *representatives,* not the singular *one.*)

Note: An easy way to find the antecedent of the relative pronoun in this type of sentence is to shift the sentence elements:

Of the letters *that were* on my desk, one has disappeared. (It now becomes obvious that the antecedent of the relative pronoun *that* is *letters.*)

Of those candidates *who are* applying for the position, here is one.

Of the representatives *who are* attending the meeting, one is wanted on the telephone.

But when the word *only* precedes *one* in this type of sentence, the singular pronoun *one* is considered to be the antecedent of the relative pronoun.

Here is *one* of the candidates *who are* eligible.

Here is the *only one* of the candidates *who is* eligible. (Notice the difference in number of the relative pronoun *who*—and its verb—in these two sentences.)

Robbins is the *only one* of the employees *who is* receiving an award.

This is the *only one* of the e-mails *that has* not yet been answered.

Who, that, or *which* may be used to refer to a collective noun. When the members of the group act, or are considered, as a unit, either *that* or *which* should be used—*that* is usually preferred if the group comprises persons rather than things. *Who* is used when the persons comprising a group act, or are considered, individually.

> The mayor reports that there *is* a *group* of citizens *that* is critical of the city's long-range plan. (Acting as a unit—*that* is used because the group is composed of persons, not things.)

> A *group* of regulations *which* we favor is on the agenda. (Acting as a unit—composed of things.)

> We have heard from an *association* of homeowners *who feel* strongly opposed to the present zoning regulations. (Considered individually—*who* signals this point.)

Subjects Joined by *And*

When two or more subjects are joined by *and*, whether the subjects are singular or plural, they form a compound subject that is considered plural.

> The *date and the time* of the meeting *have* not been decided.

> The *director and the assistants are* holding *their* weekly staff meeting.

> The *letters, reports, and other papers are* on the table where you left *them*.

> *Moses and I will* deliver *our* report in person.

Phrases or clauses serving as subjects follow the same rule: When two or more phrases or clauses serving as the subject of a sentence are joined by *and*, the resulting compound subject is considered plural.

> *Rising early in the morning* and *taking a walk before breakfast make* a person feel invigorated all day.

> *That your work is usually done satisfactorily* and *that you are usually prompt are* the factors I considered in excusing your recent conduct.

Exception: When the subjects joined by *and* refer to the same person or object or represent a single idea, the whole subject is considered singular.

> *Ham and eggs is* a traditional American breakfast.

> The *growth and development* of our country *is* described in this book.

We indicate to the reader, *by using the article or personal pronoun* before each member of the compound subject, whether we see the subject as a single idea or as different ideas.

> *My teacher and friend helps* me with my problems. (one person)

> *My teacher and my friend help* me with my problems. (two people)

> *The secretary and treasurer* of the committee *has* arrived.

> *The secretary and the treasurer* of the committee *have* arrived

Subjects Joined by *Or* or *Nor*

When singular subjects are joined by *or* or *nor,* the subject is considered singular.

> *Neither the principal nor the assistant principal knows* that *he* is scheduled to attend the meeting. *One or* the *other* of them has to go.

> Neither *love nor money is* sufficient to buy such devotion.

> Neither *heat nor cold nor sun nor wind affects* this material.

> A *fax or an e-mail* arrives immediately.

When one singular and one plural subject are joined by *or* or *nor,* the subject closer to the verb determines the number of the verb.

When the subjects joined by *or* or *nor* are of different persons, the subject nearer the verb determines its person. This construction, though grammatically correct, will almost always result in awkward sentences.

> I was told that *she or you were* to be responsible.
> I was told that *you or she was* to be responsible.

Rewritten:
I was told that either *she was* to be responsible or *you were.*

Do you think either *I or you are* being considered?
Do you think either *you or I am* being considered?

Rewritten:
Do you think that *you are* being considered, or that *I am?*
Do you think that *either* of us *is* being considered?

Subjects Joined by *And/Or*

When both of the subjects joined by *and/or* are plural, you should have no particular problem. The subject is considered plural, and all verbs and pronouns referring to it must be plural.

The coaches *and/or* their players *were* present at the dinner.

It is when both subjects are singular, or when one subject is singular and the other plural, that the problem arises. The number of the subject depends upon the interpretation we give the connective. If we consider *and/or* to have the force of *and,* the subject is plural.

The president *and/or (and)* the assistant *are* responsible for having the document signed.

These letters *and/or (and)* any supplementary material *are* due by the end of the week.

If we consider *and/or* to have the force of *or* (the usual interpretation), the subject nearer the verb controls.

The attorney *and/or (or)* his client *is* required to be present in court when *his* case is called.

These forms *and/or (or)* any explanatory statement *is* due by April 15.

The taxpayer *and/or (or)* the accountants *are* required to file before the date set.

Most grammarians discourage the use of *and/or* in letters not only because it is legalistic and overly formal but also because it is inexact. Your writing will be clearer if you substitute either *and* or *or* for *and/or*. Even if we need the whole of the idea expressed by *and/or*, we can say it more clearly as "the coach or his player or both."

Shifts in Number or Person

Once you establish a word as either singular or plural, keep it the same throughout the sentence. Be sure that all verbs and all pronouns referring to that word agree with it in number.

NOT: A *person needs* someone to turn to when *they are* in trouble. *(Person* is singular; therefore, the use of the plural pronoun *they* is an incorrect shift.)

BUT: A *person needs* someone to turn to when *he is* in trouble.

Note: Although the shift is corrected, using *he* as a generic pronoun is considered sexist usage. To avoid this problem, use the plural.

People need someone to turn to when *they are* in trouble.

NOT: When *one* has had a hard day at the office, it is important that *they* be able to relax in the evening. *(One* is singular; the singular pronoun *one* should be used to refer to it.)

BUT: When *one* has had a hard day at the office, it is important that *one* be able to relax in the evening.

Be consistent: If you decide that a collective is singular, keep it singular throughout the sentence—use a singular verb to agree with it and a singular pronoun to refer to it. If you establish the collective as plural, see that the verb and the pronoun are plural.

The committee *has* announced *its* decision. (Singular—acting as a unit)

The committee *have* adjourned and gone to *their* homes. (Plural—acting individually)

Our staff *is* always glad to offer *its* advice and assistance. (Singular—acting as a unit)

Our staff *are* assigned as liaison *officers* to the several operating divisions. (Plural—acting individually)

The number of insurance claims processed this year *is* larger than that processed last year. (Using "the" before "number" signals the reader that you consider the items as a unit.)

A number of claims *have* been processed this month. (Using "a" before "number" signals that you are referring to the items individually.)

Most indefinite pronouns are singular and require singular verbs and pronouns. To avoid sexist language, rewrite the sentence in the plural.

NOT: *Has anyone* turned in *their* book report? (The indefinite pronoun *anyone* takes both a singular verb and a singular pronoun.)

BUT: *Has anyone* turned in *his* or *her* book report?

OR: *Have any* of the students turned in *their* book report?

Avoid shifting the person of pronouns referring to the same antecedent.

NOT: When *one* is happy, it often seems as if everyone around *you* is happy, too. *(One* is third person; *you* is second person.)

BUT: When *one* is happy, it often seems as if everyone around *one* is happy, too.

NOT: As the *ship* entered *her* berth, *its* huge gray shadow seemed to swallow us.

BUT: As the *ship* entered *its* berth, *its* huge gray shadow seemed to swallow us.

OR: As the *ship* entered *her* berth, *her* huge gray shadow seemed to swallow us.

Structure Problems

Usually it's easy for us to identify the subject or antecedent and determine its number and person. But occasionally a puzzling sentence comes along. The subject is there, but something in the structure of the sentence confuses us and makes us believe that another word is the subject.

Verb Precedes Subject

When the verb precedes the subject in the sentence (either in a question or in a declarative sentence), locate the *true* subject and make the verb agree with it.

Are the *file cabinet and the bookcase* in this room? (The *file cabinet and the bookcase* are . . .)

Walking down the hall *are* the *paralegals* we are waiting for.

From these books *come some* of our best *ideas*.

To us *falls* the *task* of supporting the team.

Among those attending *were* two former *presidents* of the organization.

Where, here, and *there,* when introducing a sentence, do not influence the number or person of the verb. In such sentences, find the real subject and make the verb agree with it.

Where *are* the individual *meetings* to be held?
Where *is* the *text* filed?

Here *are* the *reports* for which we were waiting.
Here *is* the *report* for which we were waiting.

There *are* two *books* on the table.
There *is* a *book* on the table.

What, who, which, the interrogative pronouns, do not affect the number of the verb. Again, find the subject *of* the sentence and make the verb agree with it.

What *is* the *status of* the players' strike?
What *are* your *recommendations* on this problem?

Who *is* going to accompany you to the show?
Who, in this group, *are* members of your club?

Which *is* the *report* that the engineer means?
Which *are* the *standards* that we are to apply?

The expletive *it* or *there* introduces the verb and stands for the real subject, which comes later in the clause. The expletive *it* requires a singular verb, even when the real subject is plural. Following the expletive *there,* the verb is singular or plural according to the subject which follows it.

It is solutions we are looking for, not problems. (Even though the real subject of *is, solutions,* is plural, the verb is singular to agree with the expletive.)

It is doubtful that she will start today. (The clause *that she will start today* is the subject of the verb *is.*)

There *are* enclosed five copies of the pamphlet you requested.

There *is* attached a letter from a friend, requesting additional copies of the book.

Avoid confusing the reader by using the expletive *it* and the personal pronoun *it* in the same sentence.

NOT: I haven't read the paper yet; *it* has been hard for me to find time for *it.* (The first it is the expletive; the second *it* is a personal pronoun referring to *paper.)*

BUT: I haven't read the paper yet; I haven't been able to find time for *it.*

Words Intervene Between Subject and Verb

The presence of explanatory or parenthetical phrases, or other modifiers, between the subject and verb does not change the number or person of the subject. Locate the real subject of the sentence and make the verb agree with it.

The most common source of error is to mistake a prepositional phrase for the subject of the verb when the prepositional phrase immediately follows the subject.

The *officers* of the corporation *are* elected annually.

The *result* of the experiments *leads* to a new theory about genes.

The *letter* with its several attachments *was* received this morning.

The *amount* shown, plus interest, *is* due within 30 days.

The *letter* with its several attachments *was* received this morning.

Our *letters,* like our speech, *are* indications of our knowledge of English.

The *report,* including extensive notes on the background research, *was* well received.

No one but those present *knows* of this information.

Subject and Predicate Differ in Number

After forms of the verb *to be* we often find a construction (called the *predicate nominative*) that means the same thing as the subject. When the predicate nominative differs in number from the subject, the verb must agree with the element that precedes it (the subject).

Our main *problem is* writing complete essays and keeping them short enough for fast reading.

Writing complete essays and keeping them short enough for fast reading *are* our main problem.

As always, the *question was* sufficient team players.

As always, *sufficient* team players *were* the question.

Special Problems of Pronoun Reference

Ambiguous Antecedents

Do not use forms of the same pronoun to refer to different antecedents.

NOT: The teacher told Mr. Johnson that *he* thought *his* work was improving. (Does the teacher think that his own work is improving, or that Mr. Johnson's work is improving?)

BUT: Mr. Johnson was told by his teacher that his work was improving.

When it seems that the pronoun can logically refer to either of two antecedents, be sure that the reference is obvious.

NOT: The coach told Sonia that *she* would have to make *her* proposed trip to Boston in June. (The pronouns *she* and *her* can refer to either *coach* or *Sonia.* The meaning may be apparent when this sentence is placed in context, but rewriting will insure clarity.)

COULD MEAN: Although Sonia had planned to travel to Boston in May, the coach asked *her* to postpone the trip until June.

OR: Since the coach is planning a trip to Boston in June, she was obliged to decline Sonia's invitation to speak at the sports conference.

Place the pronoun as close as possible to its antecedent to avoid ambiguity or confusion.

NOT: A young graduate can readily find a job *that* is skilled in data processing. (Although the pronoun *that* refers to *graduate,* its placement makes it appear to refer to *job.*)

BUT: A *young graduate that* is skilled in data processing can readily find a job.

NOT: The letter is on the table *that* we received yesterday. (If it was the letter that was received yesterday, not the table, this sentence should read: The *letter that* we received yesterday is on the table.)

Antecedent in Subordinate Construction

If the antecedent of the pronoun is in a subordinate construction, the reference is likely to be vague. Be careful of antecedents in the possessive case or in prepositional phrases. There may be a more prominent word in the sentence to which the pronoun may seem to refer.

NOT: The copies of these plans were not signed by the drafters, so we are sending *them* back. (What are we sending back? The copies, the plans, or the drafters?)

BUT: We are send back the copies of the plans because they were not signed by the drafters.

NOT: When you have finished the last chapter of the book, please return *it* to the library. (We can assume that the pronoun *it* refers to *book*. The more prominent noun "chapter" is the word to which *it* would grammatically refer, even though logically *it* refers to the noun in the subordinate construction.)

BUT: Please return the *book* to the library when you have finished *its* (the) last chapter.

Implied Antecedents

As a general rule, the antecedent of a pronoun must appear in the sentence—not merely be implied. And the antecedent should be a specific word, not an idea expressed in a phrase or clause. *It, which, this,* and *that* are the pronouns that most often lead our meaning astray. Any of these pronouns may refer to an idea expressed in a preceding passage if the idea and the reference are *unmistakably clear.* But too often the idea that is unmistakably clear to the writer is nowhere to be found when the reader looks for it.

NOT: Although the doctor operated at once, *it* was not a success, and the patient died. (The pronoun *it* refers to the idea of *operation,* which is implied but not expressed in the first part of the sentence.)

BUT: Although the doctor performed the *operation* at once, *it* was not a success, and the patient died.

OR: Although the doctor operated at once, the *operation* was not a success, and the patient died.

NOT: Ms. Roberts has recently been promoted. *This* brings her greater responsibility and will probably mean longer hours for her. (Although it is pretty obvious that *this* refers to Ms. Roberts' promotion, the word *promotion* does not appear in the sentence.)

BUT: Ms. Roberts has recently received a *promotion*. *This* brings her greater responsibility and will probably mean longer hours for her.

Vague Reference

The usage illustrated below—the impersonal use of *it*, *they*, and *you*—is not incorrect. But using these impersonal pronouns tends to produce vague, wordy sentences.

NOT: In the manual *it* says to make three copies. (Who says?)
BUT: The manual says to make three copies.

NOT: In the letter *it* says he will be here on Thursday.
BUT: The letter says he will be here on Thursday.
OR: He says, in his letter, that he will be here on Thursday.

NOT: *They* say we are in for a cold, wet winter.
BUT: The almanac predicts a cold, wet winter.

NOT: From this report *you* can easily recognize the cause of the accident.
BUT: From this report *one* can easily recognize the cause of the accident. (The first example is correct if the writer is addressing his remarks to a specific person.)
OR: The cause of the accident can be easily recognized from this report.

Quiz

To review your understanding of agreement and reference, take the following quiz.

Directions: Read the following sentences for errors involving agreement and reference. If you find an error rewrite the sentence. If the sentence is correct, write "correct."

1. The audience always applauds the dramatic solo.

2. A group of residents which live in the apartment complex recommended changes in parking rules.

3. Trash disposal and parking always produces complaints.

4. A letter carrier is blamed when they deliver mail to the wrong address.

5. The residents expect that your mail will be delivered correctly.

6. Has the letter and packages been delivered?

7. There are the deliveries we have been waiting for.

8. Biology or physics is required to graduate.

9. The students told the teachers that they believed the exams were fair.

10. Upon entering the building, the dean's office is on the left.

11. In this editorial, it argues that tax increases are unnecessary.

12. The title of Trevor's novel it is "The Story of Lucy Gault."

13. Here are the shelves on which a new book can be found.

14. What did the critics says about this book?

15. The review, including discussion of the novel's characters, were favorable.

Answers and Explanations

1. Correct. The audience always *applauds* the dramatic solo. The members of the group, the *audience*, is considered as a unit; the verb must be singular.

2. A group of residents *that* live in the apartment complex recommended changes in parking rules. Use *that*, not *which* when a collective noun refers to a group of *people* referred to as a unit.

3. Trash disposal and parking always *produce* complaints. When two or more subjects of the same verb are joined by *and*, use a plural verb.

4. *Letter carriers are* blamed when they deliver mail to the wrong address. The original sentence has a singular form, *letter carrier*, as the antecedent of a plural pronoun, *they*.

5. The residents expect that their mail will be delivered correctly. Keep the person of words in a sentence consistent. *Residents* is third person. Thus, the third person possessive pronoun should be used.

6. *Have* the letter and packages been delivered? Even though the subject follows the verb, *letter and packages* is a compound subject that requires a plural verb.

7. Correct. There *are* the deliveries we have been waiting for. *Deliveries*, the subject of *are*, is plural. The word *there* does not influence the number or person of a verb.

8. Correct. *Biology or physics* is required to graduate. Compound subjects joined by *or* take a singular verb.

9. The students believed that the exams were fair and told that to the teachers. OR: The teachers believed the exams were fair and told the students so. The original sentence is ambiguous. Who told whom that the exams were fair?

10. *When one enters the building*, the dean's office is on the left. In the original sentence, the office is entering the building.

11. *This editorial argues* that tax increases are unnecessary. Avoid the vague use of *it*. In this sentence, *it* can be omitted because *editorial* is the subject of the verb.

12. The title of Trevor's novel *is* "The Story of Lucy Gault." *Title* is the subject of the verb. *It* is unnecessary.

13. Correct. Here *are* the *shelves* on which a new book can be found. When *here* introduces a sentence, it does not influence the number of the verb. *Shelves* is the subject of *are*.

14. What did the critics *say* about the book? Do not be confused when words come between parts of the verb. The subject, *critics*, comes between the parts of the verb, *did say*.

15. The review, including discussion of the novel's characters, *was* favorable. Do not be confused by phrases which come between the subject and the verb. Modifiers do not change the relation of the subject and verb. *Review* is singular; the verb should be singular even though the word right before the verb, *characters*, is plural.

4
TENSE OF VERBS AND VERBALS

The verb is the backbone of the sentence. It is the word that tells what action is taking place or what condition exists. The verb puts life into the sentence; without it there *is* no sentence—just a group of words lined up with nothing to do, with no place to go. Give such words a verb, and they spring into action.

Since verbs are so important, it is to our advantage to get as much use from them as we can. To do this, we must get better acquainted with them. We must learn enough about verbs, for example, to know what happens when we use an *active* instead of a *passive* verb. For when a verb is *active* the whole sentence takes on life and vigor—the subject is busy *doing something;* when a verb is *passive,* the movement of the sentence slows down—the subject isn't *doing* anything, simply waiting passively while something is *being done to it by someone.*

And we must learn more about *verbals,* those interesting but confusing words that come from verbs. They are interesting (and valuable) because, in the hands of the experienced writer, they make wanting more effective. They are confusing because, although they come from verbs and are like verbs in many ways, they can't do the work of verbs; instead, they function as other parts of speech—as nouns or as adjectives, for example.

Becoming more familiar with verbs and verbals will mean reviewing their peculiar characteristics *(properties)* and the way verbs change form to indicate these characteristics.

Two of the five properties of verbs—*number* and *person*—we discussed in the previous chapter. Two others—*mood* and *voice* we will discuss in the next chapter. In this chapter we will discuss *tense.*

Tenses of Verbs

Tense indicates time. We know that, as their main function, verbs describe an action or a state of being on the part of the subject. But verbs also tell *when* the action took place or *when* the state existed. This property of verbs is called tense.

Tense tells the time of the action from the point of view of the writer or speaker. Take the act of *walking* as an example.

If we say, "I *am walking* to work," we are looking, from the standpoint of the *present* time, at an action that is taking place now.

If we say, "I *walked* to work last Tuesday," we are looking, again from the standpoint of the *present* time, at an action that happened in the past (last Tuesday).

If we say, "If I walk to work tomorrow, I *shall have walked* to work every day this week," we are placing ourselves in the future (tomorrow) and speaking from that point of view.

If we say, "I told him yesterday that I *had walked* to work," we are speaking, from the point of view of some time in the past (yesterday), of an action that was completed even before that "past time."

English has six tenses: three simple tenses *(present, past,* and *future)* in which an action may be considered as simply occurring, and three compound—called *perfect*—tenses in which an action may be considered as completed. (To be *perfected* means to be *completed*.)

PRESENT TENSE:	I walk, he walks
PRESENT PERFECT TENSE:	I have walked, he has walked
PAST TENSE:	I walked, he walked
PAST PERFECT TENSE:	I had walked, he had walked
FUTURE TENSE:	I shall walk, he will walk
FUTURE PERFECT TENSE:	I shall have walked, he will have walked

Each of the six tenses has a companion form—the *progressive* form. As its name indicates, the progressive says that the action named by the verb is a continued or progressive action. The progressive consists of the present participle (the *-ing* form of the verb, that is, *walking*) plus the proper form of the verb *to be*. The progressive forms of the verb *to walk* are:

PRESENT TENSE: I am walking, he is walking

PRESENT PERFECT TENSE: I have been walking, he has been walking

PAST TENSE: I was walking, he was walking

PAST PERFECT TENSE: I had been walking, he had been walking

FUTURE TENSE: I shall be walking, he will be walking

FUTURE PERFECT TENSE: I shall have been walking, he will have been walking

We indicate tense by changing the verb itself or by combining forms of the verb with auxiliary verbs. The verb forms that we use to indicate tense are called the *principal parts*. The principal parts of a verb are:

THE INFINITIVE OR PRESENT TENSE: talk, write

THE PAST TENSE: talked, wrote

THE PAST PARTICIPLE: talked, written

The past participle is always used with an auxiliary verb, like *have*, *has*, or *had: they have talked, he has written.*

A fourth principal part, which is the same for all verbs, is the *present participle*. It consists of the present form plus *-ing: talking, writing.*

Verbs are classified as *regular* (or *weak)* and *irregular* (or *strong),* according to the way in which their principal parts are formed. Regular verbs form their past tense and past participles by the addition of *-ed* to the infinitive:

INFINITIVE	PAST TENSE	PAST PARTICIPLE
talk	talked	talked
help	helped	helped
tax	taxed	taxed

The principal parts of irregular verbs are formed by changes in the verb itself:

INFINITIVE	PAST TENSE	PAST PARTICIPLE
see	saw	seen
say	said	said
go	went	gone

Consult a standard dictionary when you are not sure of the principal parts of a verb. This area of usage is changing, and a verb that was irregular yesterday may be regular (or both regular and irregular) today.

The following verbs illustrate this change:

INFINITIVE	PAST TENSE	PAST PARTICIPLE
dive	dived (formally dove)	dived
prove	proved	proved (formally proven)

The principal parts of a verb are given in a dictionary at the beginning of the listing for that particular verb. If no entry is given, the past tense and the past participle are formed by the addition of -*ed*. If the verb is irregular, or if it presents some difficulty of spelling, the past forms are given.

Specific Use of Tenses

Present Tense

The present tense is used primarily to describe an action that is happening in the present or a state that exists at the present time.

I *am* a member of that club.

I *am running* for the office of treasurer.

A special form of the present tense, called the *emphatic present,* uses *do* as an auxiliary verb. This tense form merely adds emphasis to a statement.

PRESENT: I may work slowly, but I *work* accurately.

EMPHATIC: I may work slowly, but I *do work* accurately.

Some functions of the present tense used less frequently require special mention:

(1) The present tense is used to indicate habitual or customary action, regardless of the tense of other verbs in the same sentence.

Whenever he *makes* a mistake, he *blames* someone else.
I always *eat* in the cafeteria, and had a salad on Tuesday.
She *leaves* the office promptly at 4:30 every day.

(2) The present tense may express a universal or relatively permanent truth, such as scientific or historical fact.

I was taught that two and two *are* four.
Atlanta *is* the capital of Georgia.

(3) The present tense may be used to make more vivid the description of some past action. This usage is known as the *historical* present; it is more common in narrative.

As Bob *is leaving* the house the telephone *rings.* He *turns* back into the house and *picks* up the receiver. It *is* his sister calling.

Either the historical present tense or the past tense may be used to restate or summarize the facts from a book, report, letter, or similar document.

The author *describes* (or *described*) the events leading him to his conclusion. He *begins* (or *began*) with …

In his letter of January 24, Ms. Saroyan *states* (or *stated*) that she is (or *was*) unable to fill our order.

A word of caution: When you use the historical present, guard against unconsciously shifting to the past tense without cause.

NOT: The author *describes* the events leading him to his conclusion. He *began* with ...

BUT: He *begins* with ...

(4) The present tense is often used to express future time:

(a) either with the help of a modifier fixing the time

Tomorrow I *go* (or *will go*) to Chicago.
She *arrives* (or *will arrive*) Sunday for a week's visit.

(b) or in a subordinate clause introduced by *if, when, after, before, until, as soon as,* etc.

As soon as he *arrives,* we shall begin the meeting.

He will not be able to complete the report until I *give* him the figures.

Present Perfect Tense

The present perfect tense describes:

(1) an action just completed at the present time:

The president *has* just *arrived* at the meeting.

I *have worked* in the garden this afternoon.

(2) an action begun in the past and continuing into the present:

I *have been* with this company for seven years. (and still am)

He *has held* that job for three years. (and still does)

Note: In speaking, avoid using the dialectal expression, "I *am* in Houston for 16 years," instead of "I *have been* in Houston for 16 years."

Past Tense

The past tense describes an action or state of being as having occurred some time in the past.

I *received* your letter this morning.

She *left* the office ten minutes ago.

I *was giving* the student their instructions when the dean *entered.*

Like the present tense, the past tense has an emphatic form, formed by the auxiliary *did.*

> PAST TENSE: I *gave* him the letter, even though he says he can't find it.
>
> EMPHATIC: I *did give* him the letter, even though he says he can't find it.

Past Tense vs. Past Participle

The past tense form is used *only* for the past tense. Use the past participle, not the past tense, with auxiliaries to form other tenses. (The past tense and past participle forms of regular verbs are the same; it is the irregular verbs that cause trouble here.)

> NOT: I *have went* to the movies this afternoon.
> BUT: I *went* to the movies this afternoon. *past tense*
> OR: I *have gone* to the movies.

Past Tense vs. Present Perfect Tense

Remember that the present perfect tense describes an action which may have started some time in the past but which continues up to, and perhaps through, the present.

I *worked* there for 15 years. *past tense*

I *have worked* there for 15 years. *present perfect tense* (The first sentence, by the use of the past tense, implies that I no longer work there. The second sentence says that I still work there.)

I *lost* my notes of the meeting. *past tense* (I lost them some time in the past; I may or may not have found them.)

I *have lost* my notes of the meeting. *present perfect tense* (The use of the present perfect extends the action into the present; therefore, it is safe to assume that the notes are still missing.)

Past Perfect Tense

The past perfect tense indicates that the action or condition it describes was completed (perfected) earlier than some other action that also occurred in the past. We use this tense when we need to show that two actions happened at different times in the past.

He *had finished* his breakfast before I *came* downstairs.
(past perfect)   (past)

I *had* mailed the letter when she *called*.
(past perfect)   (past)

Past Tense vs. Past Perfect Tense

Distinguish carefully between these two tenses: Remember that the past tense can describe an event that happened at any time in the past but that the past perfect tense must describe an event that happened *before* another event in the past. The sentences following may help clarify this usage.

When I *came* back from lunch, she *finished* the letter. (Both verbs are in the past tense; therefore, both actions happened at approximately the same time in the past.)

When I *came* back from lunch, she *had finished* the letter. (Again, both actions occurred in the past, but the use of the past perfect *had finished* tells us that this action was completed before the other action.)

We *discovered* that a detective *was following* us. (Both actions happened at the same time in the past.)

We *discovered* that a detective *had been following us.* (He had been following us some time before we discovered it.)

Future Tense

The future tense is used to indicate that an action will take place some time in the future or that a state or condition will exist some time in the future.

I *shall not be* at the game Friday.
He *will be waiting* for me after work.

Note: Distinction between *shall—will,* and *should—would*

In formal writing there is a distinction between these words. This distinction has almost disappeared in both speech and writing except for extremely formal situations such as legal documents, ceremonial speeches, and some political texts. There, the simple future tense is formed by the use of *shall* (or *should*) in the first person and *will* (or *would*) in the second and third person.

To express the will or determination of the speaker that something is to be done, use *will* or *would* in the first person and *shall* or *should* in second and third person.

(1) The teacher *will* furnish this information. (a simple statement of fact)
(2) The teacher *shall* furnish this information. (This is mandatory; the teacher *must* furnish the information.)

Simple future (expressing probable future action):

I will (or) shall	we will (or) shall	I would (or) should	we would (or) should
you will	you will	you would	you would
he will	they will	he would	they would
she will		she would	

Emphatic future (expressing the determination or the will of the speaker):

I will	we will	I would	we would
you shall	you shall	you should	you should
he shall	they shall	he should	they should
she shall		she should	

Future Perfect Tense

The future perfect tense names an action or condition that will be completed by some specified time in the future.

I *will have been* with this company for 10 years on next Tuesday.
He *will have finished* that project by April 10.

Sequence of Tense

Knowing how *to form* the various tenses is not enough, we must also know how *to use* tense logically in our sentences. To do this, we must understand *sequence* of tense.

What is sequence of tense: It is the logical time relation (expressed by tense) between the verbs in a sentence or passage. It is the way we tell our reader in what order events occurred.

Tense of Verbs in Principal Clauses

The verbs in principal clauses should be in the same tense if they refer to the same thing. Be consistent in your point of view. When you describe a series of actions that occurred at the same time, keep the verbs in the same tense. But if you interrupt the series with an action that happened earlier or later, be sure to change tense to show the time relation of this new action.

Tense of Verbs in Subordinate Clauses

The verb in the principal clause is taken as a starting point. The tenses of all verbs in subordinate clauses are determined by whether the action they describe takes place before, after, or at the same time as the action described by the verb in the principal clause.

(1) If the verb in the principal clause is in the present or future tense, the verbs in the subordinate clauses *are not restricted to* those two tenses but may be in any tense.

I hope Anna *is* in the office.
I hope Anna *was* in the office when you called.
I hope Anna *will be* in the office when we arrive.

(2) If the verb in the principal clause is in the past or past perfect tense, the verbs in the subordinate clauses must be in some tense that denotes past time.

> I *thought* that they *were visiting* you this week.
> I *thought* that they *had been visiting* you all summer.
> I *thought* that they *had visited* you the previous year.

Exception: The present tense is preferred for the verb in a subordinate clause stating a universal truth or a statement of fact, even if the verb in the principal clause is in some other tense.

> The text *tells* me that Beijing *is* the capital of China.
> Han *told* me that Beijing *is* the capital of China.
> Ancient civilizations *didn't believe* that the world *is* round.

(3) In clauses of result or purpose (introduced by such conjunctions as *in order that, so that*)

(a) if the verb in the principal clause is in the past or past perfect tense, use one of the past auxiliaries (*might, could, would*) in the subordinate clause.
The owner *gave* (or *had given*) me a pass so that I *could* get into the stadium.

(b) if the verb in the principal clause is in the present or the future tense, use a present auxiliary (*can, may*) in the subordinate clause.
The owner *will give* me a pass so that I can get into the stadium.

Tenses of Verbals

In the previous sections we have explored the tense of "finite" verbs—those verbs that perform the functions usually associated with verbs. But finite verbs are not the only verb forms involved in our use of tense. Verbals, too, need to be considered in any discussion of tense and tense sequence.

Even though the three kinds of verbals—gerund, participles, and infinitives—do not function as verbs, they do retain some of the characteristics of verbs. One of these characteristics is "tense." Participles have three tenses; gerunds and infinitives, two.

Gerunds

The gerund has two tense forms: *present and perfect.*

PRESENT: talking, writing

PERFECT: having talked, having written

> *Writing* letters is hard work. (*Writing* is the gerund; *letters is* its object. The gerund phrase is the subject of the sentence.)
>
> It is a treat to watch Kyle's *swimming.* (*Kyle's* is the subject of the gerund *swimming.*)

Note: The subject of a gerund should be in the possessive case. Notice this usage in the sentence above and in two of the examples below.

> The student's *writing* won first prize. (The gerund *writing* and its subject *student's* form a gerund phrase which serves as the subject of the sentence.)
>
> Careful, courteous *driving* is the trademark of a mature driver. (The gerund and its two modifiers form a gerund phrase which is the subject of the sentence.)
>
> She was honored for her *having done* such an outstanding job. (The perfect gerund *having done* and its subject *her* forms a gerund phrase which is the object of the preposition *for.*)
>
> *Our not having arrived* on time meant that we missed the first half of the program. (The gerund phrase is the subject of the sentence.)

Participle

The participle has three tense forms: present, past, and perfect.

PRESENT PARTICIPLE: talking, writing
PAST PARTICIPLE: talked, written
PERFECT PARTICIPLE: having talked, having written

The person *talking* on the telephone is my editor. (The participle *talking* modifies *person*.)

The article, *beautifully written,* appeared in last week's *Time.* (The participle *written,* plus its modifier *beautifully,* modifies *article*.)

The memo, *having been drafted* and *reviewed,* was ready for printing. (The participles *having been drafted* and *reviewed* modify *memo*.)

Infinitives

The infinitive has two tense forms: the present and the perfect.

PRESENT: to talk, to write
PERFECT: to have talked, to have written.

To recognize and *define* the problem is our first step.

Hughes is thought *to have written* that diary.

Verbals in Sentence Fragments

Sentence fragments (or fragmentary sentences) are parts of sentences erroneously punctuated as complete sentences. A common type of fragmentary sentence contains one or more verbals but no finite verb in the main clause. Learn to distinguish between verbals and finite verbs so that you can avoid writing this type of fragmentary sentence. Remember, mere length does not make a sentence—we need a verb.

FRAGMENT: Sentences of from 1 to 5 years in prison imposed upon six offenders arrested in connection with seizure of a large illicit drug lab set up in a tobacco barn in southern Maryland.

CORRECTED: Sentences of from I to 5 years in prison *were imposed…*

FRAGMENT: Your memorandum dated March 4, 1983,

requesting information about the availability of certain training materials and about the plans for distribution of these materials.

CORRECTED: Your memorandum dated March 4, 1983 *requested...*

Another common type of fragment error occurs when a main clause is preceded or followed by a verbal phrase, and the verbal is written as complete sentence. A punctuation change can correct this error. But rewriting the verbal as a subordinate clauses makes the meaning clearer and is a better way to revise such mistakes.

NOT: Having lost his credit card. Joseph worried a dishonest person might find it.

BUT: Having lost his credit card, Joseph worried a dishonest person might find it.

OR: Because he lost his credit card, Joseph worried dishonest person might find. it.

NOT: Nina rushed to get dressed. Being that she had forgotten to set the alarm.

BUT: Nina rushed to get dressed since she had forgotten to set the alarm.

Tense Sequence with Verbals

Verbals cannot by themselves indicate the exact time of an action. They can express time only in relation to the time of the main verb in the sentence. Verbals show that an action happened at the same time as the action of the main verb or that it happened at an earlier time.

Participles

Only two forms of the participle—the present and the perfect— are of interest to us here, since the past participle is usually used as part of a verb phrase.

The present participle refers to action happening at the same time as the action of the main verb.

Entering the office the applicant *confirms* the appointment. (The main verb is in the present tense; therefore, the present participle *entering* carries the idea of present time.)

Entering the office the applicant *confirmed* the appointment. (With the change in the tense of the main verb to the past, we also change the time of the participle change automatically.)

The perfect participle refers to action occurring *before* the action of the main verb.

Having finished the repairs, the plumber *is preparing* to leave.

Having finished the repairs, the plumber *was preparing* to leave.

Study the following pairs of sentences for the use of the present and perfect participles. Remember, the present participle names action occurring at the same time as the action of the main verb; the perfect participle names action occurring before that of the main verb.

Being late for work, I ran up the stairs.

Having been late for work, I decided to stay and finish the report after hours.

Intending to return immediately, I left the door open when I went out.

Having intended to return immediately, I was disappointed at having to be away so long.

Selling their house, they prepared to move to Florida.

Having sold their house, they were free to leave.

Infinitives

The present infinitive names an action occurring at the same time as the action of the main verb.

The sentences below all contain present infinitives. Notice that we must depend upon the tense of the main verb to tell us the time of the action of both the main verb and the infinitive.

I *am trying to finish* this report today. (Both actions are happening in the present.)

I *was trying to finish* the report before they asked for it. (Both actions happened at the same time in the past.)

I *will try to finish* the report by the end of the day. (Both actions will happen at the same time in the future.)

I *am writing to request* three copies of your latest catalog. (Both actions happen in the present.)

I *wrote to request* three copies of their catalog. (Both happened at the same time in the past.)

I *will write* tomorrow *to request* a copy of their catalog. (Both actions will happen at the same future time.)

The present infinitive also expresses future time, sometimes with the help of a time modifier.

I *hope to attend* the meeting next Tuesday. (I hope *now* to attend in the future.)

I *plan to write* about the demonstration. (I plan *now* to write in the future.)

She *expected to be* here by today. (She expected *in the past* to be here at some future time.)

He *had hoped to win* the trophy. (He had hoped *in the past* to win at some future time.)

The perfect infinitive expresses action occurring *before* that of the main verb.

I am glad *to have been* of assistance. (I am glad *now* to have been of assistance in the past.)

I am honored *to have known* such a person. (I am honored *now* to have known him in the past.)

The sentences below contrast the use of the present and perfect infinitives.

> Kelly appears *to be* a military officer. (Present—he appears *now* to be an officer *now*)

> Kelly appears *to have been* a military officer. (Perfect—he appears *now* to have been an officer *in the past*)

> I was glad *to be* of service. (Present—I was glad *then* to be of service *at that time*)

> I am glad *to have been* of service. (Perfect—I am glad *now* to have been of service *in the past*)

After a verb in the past or past perfect tense, the present infinitive will usually best express your meaning. Be careful of sentences in which both the main verb and the infinitive are preceded by *has, have,* or *had.* These auxiliaries are rarely, if ever, needed in both constructions.

> NOT: I should have liked *to have seen her* when she was here.
> BUT: I should have liked *to see her* when she was here.

> NOT: I had hoped *to have shipped* the order by now.
> BUT: I had hoped *to ship* the order by now.

> NOT: We had expected *to have finished* the book by May.
> BUT: We had expected *to finish* the book by May.

Gerunds

The present tense of the gerund refers to an action happening at the present time:

> *Taking* a review course does not guarantee success.

The perfect tense of the gerund refers to an action that was completed *before* the time of the main verb.

> He *attributes* his success to *having studied* whenever possible.

Timetable

To make the meaning clear for the reader, choose the verb forms that best express the time elements involved. Use the following timetable as a quick reminder:

IS................... to express a fact or a condition existing now; to express a universal or permanent truth; to express past conditions vividly.

WAS............... to express a past or completed fact or condition.

WILL BE........... to express a future fact or condition.

IS................... with a modifier to express future time or in a subordinate clause introduced by *when, if, after, before, until,* etc.
The therapist *will be* in the meeting tomorrow.
The therapist *is* to be in the Medical Office soon.
Next Friday *is* the end of the pay period. (will be)
Next Saturday *will be* the end of the pay period. (is)
The conference *will be* held next Monday. (is)
The conference *is* to be held next Monday. (will be)

HAS/HAVE......... to express an action which still exists, or the results of which still exist.

HAD .... to express a past or completed action.
The woman says that she *has paid* her bill.
The woman said that she *had paid* her bill.
He *has worked* in the building since 1990. (still is)
He transferred here from downtown where he *had worked* for 10 years.

HAS BEEN......... to express an action which still exists, or the result of which still exists.

WAS .... to express a past or completed action.
The employee *has been working* on the entertainment committee.

The employee *was* a member of the entertainment committee.

TO BE/TO DO ... TO HAVE BEEN	to express the same time as the main verbs, or TO future time.

TO HAVE BEEN TO HAVE DONE.. TO HAVE HAD	to express time before the main verb. The survey *was thought to be* essential. (indicates same time) Lincoln *is thought* by our historians *to have been* a man of great vision. (*To have been* indicates time before the main verb.) It *would have been* unfair *to do* that. <div align="center">or</div>It *would be* unfair *to do* that.

SHOULD HAVE LIKED WOULD HAVE LIKED...	to be followed by the present instead of the past of verbs with "to." I *should have liked to see* the movie. I *would have liked to meet* you and (to) *discuss* the wedding.

BEING DOING…......................	to express the same time as the main verbs or future time.

HAVING BEEN HAVING DONE	to express time before the main verbs. There *was* some question of his *doing* the painting. There *was* some question of his *having done* the painting.

WOULD BE SHOULD BE................. COULD BE	to express the same time as the main verbs, or time after the main verbs.

WOULD HAVE BEEN

SHOULD HAVE BEEN ... to express time before the main verbs.

COULD HAVE BEEN   It *was* thought that the missing clue *could* easily *have been obtained.* (Or: could be)

They *decided* that it *would have been* worthwhile to go.

SHALL HAVE BEEN

WILL HAVE BEEN........ to express action performed before some future time and action performed before the present time.

We *shall have* the new furniture before then. (future)

The decorating *will have been* finished by now. (before present)

Quiz

Errors in tense may create illogical sentences or sentences that don't convey your meaning. Review your understanding of tense of verbs and verbals with the following quiz.

Directions: Read the following sentences looking for problems with verb tenses. If you find an error, rewrite the sentence. If the sentence is correct, write "correct."

1. The producers have went to great expense to promote the new film.

2. They have copied media campaigns that increased attendance.

3. The film begins when the main character's wife died.

4. The cast seen the film at a private screening.

5. The director's editing of the film contributed to its success.

6. Employers shall submit a form W-2 for all employees by January 31.

7. The Internal Revenue Service regulating the dates these forms are due.

8. Our accountant knew that these forms are always due on that date.

9. The company did not submit the forms on time. Being that a computer crashed and the data was lost.

10. The accountant believed that this excuses the late filing.

Answers and Explanations

1. The producers *have gone* to great expense to promote the new film. *Go* is an irregular verb. The past participle is *gone*, not *went*.

2. Correct. They *have copied* media campaigns that increased attendance. The present perfect tense describes an action just completed at the present time or an action begun in the past and continuing into the present.

3. The film begins when the main character's wife *dies*. When using the historical present tense, do not shift to the past tense unless there is a reason to do so.

4. The cast *saw* the film at a private screening. *See* is an irregular verb. The past form is *saw*, not *seen*.

5. Correct. The *director's editing* of the film contributed to its success. Use the possessive before a gerund.

6. Correct. Employers *shall* submit a form W-2 for all employees by January 31. Although the distinction between *shall* and *will* has almost disappeared, *shall* is preferred in formal context such as laws and regulations.

7. The Internal Revenue Service *regulates* the dates these forms are due. A verbal cannot serve as the verb in a sentence or an independent clause.

8. Correct. Our accountant knew that these forms *are* always due on that date. Use the present tense to express a relatively permanent truth such as a fact or a law, even if another clause in the sentence is in the past tense.

9. The company did not submit the forms on time *since* a computer crashed and the data was lost. *Being that* is a verbal phrase which cannot serve as a verb in a complete sentence.

10. The accountant believed that this *excused* the late filing. Unless there is a specific reason to, do not shift from past to present tense. Since this is the accountant's *belief*, it is not a law or a fact.

5
MOOD AND VOICE

We have seen in earlier chapters that, by its properties, a verb can tell you more than just the *name* of an action or a condition. By its *tense,* you remember, it tells the *time* of an action, and by *sequence of tense,* the time-order of several actions.

In this chapter we will discuss two more properties of the verb which you can use to make your meaning clear to the reader. These properties are *mood* and *voice.*

Mood

Mood means *manner.* Mood tells the reader the manner, or way, in which the writer regards the statement made—that is, whether it is a simple statement, a command, a wish, a statement contrary to fact, or a statement having a high degree of improbability.

You may use any one of three moods:

the *indicative*—to make a statement or to ask a question

the *imperative*—to give a command, make a request, or make a suggestion

the *subjunctive*—to express a wish, a possibility, a statement of doubt

The Indicative Mood

The *indicative mood*—used to make a statement or ask a question—is used in almost all our writing and speaking.

The conference with the producer and his director *was scheduled* for May 15.

What *is* the correct form to be used?

The Imperative Mood

The *imperative mood* expresses a command, a request, or a suggestion. The subject of an imperative sentence is ordinarily the pronoun *you* (not expressed, simply understood).

Lock the door before you leave the office.

Let us help you start this program in your school.

Please *sign* the application before returning it to us. (Note that the word *please* may be inserted with no effect on the use of the imperative, but often with a desirable effect on the reader.)

Probably the greatest mistake we make is not using the imperative mood *enough*. An order or a request stated in the imperative is usually not only more emphatic but much more quickly and easily understood.

INDICATIVE: It would be appreciated if you would forward this information promptly.

IMPERATIVE: Please forward (send) this vital information promptly.

The Subjunctive Mood

The *subjunctive mood* is used most often to express a condition contrary to fact, a wish, a supposition, or an indirect command.

Simply by changing the verb to the subjunctive mood, one can express shades of meaning that otherwise would require the insertion of several explanatory phrases.

Forms of the Subjunctive

The only recognizable forms of the subjunctive (and consequently the only ones to be discussed here) are:

(1) the form of the third person singular present (which in the indicative has an -*s* and in the subjunctive has none):

INDICATIVE: The interviewer *prepares* the report as soon as the session ends.

SUBJUNCTIVE: We suggested that the interviewer *prepare* her report immediately.

INDICATIVE: The plane usually *arrives* on schedule.

SUBJUNCTIVE: Should the plane *arrive* on schedule, we will be able to make our connection.

(2) forms of the verb *be,* which show the following differences between the indicative and the subjunctive:

INDICATIVE: I am, you are, he is, she is, we, you, they are

SUBJUNCTIVE: If *I* be   and   should *we* be
              If *you* be   should *you* be
              If *he* be   should *they* be
              If *she* be

              Note: Both *if* and *should* frequently introduce the subjunctive.

INDICATIVE: I was, you were, he was, she was, we were, you were, they were

SUBJUNCTIVE: If *I* were (difference) If *we* were (no change)
              If *you* were (no change) If *you* were (no change)
              If *he* were (difference) If *they* were (no change)
              If *she* were (difference)

Though *were* is the past form in the indicative, it is used as *present* or *future* in the subjunctive. Either *had* or *had been* is used to express past time in the subjunctive.

PRESENT SUBJUNCTIVE: If the book *were* available (now), we could finish the report.

PAST SUBJUNCTIVE: If the book *had been* available (in the past), we could have finished the report.

OR: *Had* the book been available, we could have finished the report.

PRESENT: If he *were* able to do it, I am sure he would.
PAST: *Had* she been able to do it, I am sure she would.

Uses of the Subjunctive

Most uses of the subjunctive cause little trouble. However, there are some that require you to weigh the *degree of probability* of your statement before you use the subjunctive instead of the indicative.

In the following sections, we shall list first those about which there is little question and then those that cause confusion or concern.

To express a wish not likely to be fulfilled or impossible of being realized.

I wish it *were* possible for us to approve this transaction at this time. (It is *not* possible.)

I wish they *were* here to hear your praise of their work. (They are *not* here.)

Would that I *were* able to take this trip in your place. (I am *not* able to go.)

I wish I *were* able to help you.

To express a parliamentary motion.

I move that the meeting *be* adjourned.

Resolved, that a committee *be* appointed to study this matter.

In a subordinate clause after a verb that expresses a command, a request, or a suggestion.

He asked *that* the doctor's report *be* submitted to the insurance provider.

It is recommended *that* this office *be* responsible for preparing the news release.

We suggest *that* she *be* relieved of the pressure.

It is highly desirable *that* they *be* given the authority to enter the negotiations.

To express a condition easily recognized as being contrary to fact.

If I *were* in St. Louis, I should be glad to attend.

If this *were* a simple case, we could easily agree on a solution.

If I *were* you, I should not mind the assignment.

To express a condition or supposition which you may believe to be contrary to fact or highly improbable, as contrasted with a condition or supposition which you consider to be within the realm of possibility.

Note: This is the problem area. Here, you have the obligation to tell the reader which way you see the situation—highly improbable or within the realm of possibility. You do this by your choice of the subjunctive or the indicative.

SUBJUNCTIVE: If the statement *be* true, this is a case of fraud. (The writer indicates that he thinks it is highly improbable that the statement is true.)

INDICATIVE: If the statement *is* true, this may be a case of fraud. (The writer indicates that it is quite possible that the statement may be true.)

SUBJUNCTIVE: If he *were* at the meeting, he would have spoken for the opposition. (or, *Were* he at the meeting, he would ...) (The writer tells the reader that the man is not at the meeting.)

INDICATIVE: If he *was* at the meeting, he would have been able to speak about opposing views. (Perhaps the man *was* at the meeting; the writer doesn't know).

SUBJUNCTIVE: *Had* the first payment been made in April, the car would have arrived in May. (The writer tells his reader that the payment was *not* made in April.)

INDICATIVE: If the first payment *was* made in April, the car will arrive in May. (Perhaps it was made, perhaps not—the writer doesn't know.)

After *as if* or *as though*

In formal writing and speech, *as if* and *as though* are followed by the subjunctive, since they introduce as supposition something not factual. In informal writing and speaking, the indicative is sometimes used.

FORMAL: He talked *as if* he *were* an expert on the stock market. (He's not.)

INFORMAL: She gave orders *as if* she *was* the team's coach (she wasn't)

FORMAL: This painting looks *as though* it *were* the work of an old master.

INFORMAL: The car looks *as though* it *was* in a serious accident.

Abuse of the Subjunctive

Some people, in an overzealous attempt to write correctly, use the subjunctive in all *if*-clauses. *If*-clauses are, of course, *conditional* clauses; that's what you tell your reader by your choice of the subordinate conjunction *if.* But not all *if*-clauses express thoughts that are suppositions or that are contrary to fact.

SIMPLY CONDITIONAL: If it *is* assigned to me, I shall do it. (Perhaps it *will be* assigned to me.)

CONTRARY TO FACT: If it *were* assigned to me, I would do it. (It has already been assigned to somebody else, or it is highly improbable that it will ever be assigned to me.)

Shifts in Mood

Be consistent in your point of view. Once you have decided on the mood that expresses the way you regard the message, use that mood throughout the sentence or the paragraph. A shift in mood is confusing to the reader because it indicates that you have changed your way of looking at the conditions.

NOT: It is requested that a catalog of the dishes *be* prepared and copies *should be* distributed to all buyers. *(Be is* subjunctive; *should be,* indicative.)

BUT: It is requested that a catalog of the dishes *be* prepared and that copies *be* distributed to all buyers.

NOT: Date *stamp* the quiz when it is received in the office, and then the quiz *should be sent* to the teacher. (Shift from imperative to indicative mood.)

BUT: Date *stamp* the quiz when it is received and then *send* it to the teacher.

Voice

Voice indicates whether the subject of the verb is performing or receiving the action described by the verb. There are two voices: active and passive.

If the subject is performing the action, the verb is in the active voice.

The *committee approved* our report.

The *report summarizes* the committee recommendations.

The *actor asked* the producer to have dinner.

If the subject is being acted upon, the verb is in the passive voice. (The passive form always consists of some form of *be* plus the past participle.)

Our *report was approved* by the committee.

The committee *recommendations are summarized* in the report.

The *producer was asked* by the actor to have dinner.

Uses of the Active and Passive Voices

We need to use both the active and passive voice. In technical, academic, and official writing, there has been a tendency to use the passive voice as much as possible, probably in the belief that the resulting sentences sound "more official." In an effort to put more life into writing, some writers have been using the active voice, almost to the extent of avoiding the passive voice entirely. But one extreme is as bad as the other. You need both the active and the passive voice for emphasis and for exact expression.

If you want to emphasize *who* performed an action, let your subject be the person or thing that performed the action and put your verb in the active voice. If it is relatively unimportant *who* performed the action and you want to stress instead *what action* was performed or *who was affected* by the action performed, let your subject be the person or thing "acted upon" (the receiver of the action) and put the verb in the passive voice.

> All supervisors attended the meeting. (*Supervisors* is being emphasized.)

> The meeting was attended by all supervisors. (Here *the meeting was attended* is being emphasized.)

> The INSCO Instrument Co. employs Ms. Jefferson. (This form emphasizes the company.)

> Ms. Jefferson is employed by the INSCO Instrument Co. (This form emphasizes Ms. Jefferson, not the company.)

We can't say that one voice is "correct" in certain instances and "incorrect" in others. The decision of which voice to use rests with you. You are the only one who can say which voice better suits your purpose. The active voice is, however, simpler and more direct; therefore, if either the active or the passive will serve your purpose, use the active.

> NOT: A brochure is enclosed which sets forth the dates and locations of the schools. (Passive voice. This is an example of the "untouched-by-human-hands" type of sentence.)
>
> BUT: We are enclosing a brochure which gives the dates and locations of the schools.
>
> OR: The enclosed brochure gives the dates and locations of the schools.

Shifts in Voice

Like the shift in mood, which we have discussed, a shift in voice is confusing to the readers. Even when it does not confuse them, it may distract them momentarily.

Shifts in voice—often accompanied by shifts in subject—usually occur in compound or complex sentences. Although it is not essential that all clauses in a sentence be the same in structure, any unnecessary shifts result in a disorganized sentence. Therefore, unless you have a good reason for changing, use the same subject and voice in the second clause that you used in the first.

NOT: As I searched through the files for the memorandum, the missing *report was found.* (The first subject is *I*—its verb is active; the second subject is *report*—its verb is passive.)

BUT: As I searched through the files for the memorandum, *I found* the missing report. (Subject is *I* in both clauses; both verbs are active.)

NOT: As soon as we receive the signed contract, *arrangements can be made* to pay for the merchandise. (*We* is the first subject—its verb is active; *arrangements* is the second subject—its verb is passive.)

BUT: As soon as the contract is received, arrangements can be made to pay for the merchandise. (Both verbs are in the passive voice, but have different subjects.)

OR: As soon as we receive the signed contract, *we can make* arrangements to pay for the merchandise. (Now both verbs are in the active voice and the subjects are the same.)

NOT: A summary of the minutes of the sales meeting *will be prepared,* and we will distribute copies to all personnel. (The subject of the first clause is *summary*—the verb is passive. The subject of the second clause is *we*—the verb is active.)

BUT: A summary of the minutes of the sales meeting *will be prepared* and copies *will be distributed* to all personnel. (The subjects of the two clauses are still different but the fact that the verbs are both passive makes this an improved sentence.)

OR: We will prepare a summary of the minutes of the sales meeting and (*we will*) *distribute* copies to all personnel. (*We* is the subject of both clauses; both verbs are in the active voice.)

Quiz

Because the correct choice of mood and voice differ depending on what the writer means, this quiz sets up a situation for each item. The items are related to each other.

Directions: Read the sentence describing the situation. Then decide whether answer A or answer B is the better way to word the sentence for that situation.

1. The manager wants to lease a new computer, but the company president says they can't afford the higher monthly cost. The manager says
    A. I wish I was able to sign the lease today.
    B. I wish I were able to sign the lease today.

2. The optimistic company president talks about the future.
    A. If revenues increase, we'll lease the computer.
    B. If revenues were to increase, we would lease the computer.

3. The manager argues the lease should be signed now.
    A. If I were in your position, I'd lease before prices go up.
    B. If I was in your position, I'd lease before prices go up.

4. The president does not believe prices will rise.
    A. If I was to agree, we'd sign the lease now.
    B. If I were to agree, we'd sign the lease now.

5. The company president addresses a stockholders' meeting.
    A. It appears as if I was correct in forecasting increased revenues.
    B. It appears as if I were correct in forecasting increased revenues.

6. The company president is talking to a golfing partner.
    A. It looks as though I was right.
    B. It looks as though I were right.

7. The manager tells a department head about the lease.
    A. If it was up to me, I'd lease it now.
    B. If it were up to me, I'd lease it now.

8. The department head replies.
   A. If you are able to convince the president, sign the lease.
   B. If you were able to convince the president, sign the lease.

9. The manager announces an action at a department meeting.
   A. I signed the lease for the new computer.
   B. The lease for the new computer was signed by me.

10. The manager discusses what will happen next.
    A. As soon as we receive the computer, training sessions will be scheduled.
    B. As soon as we receive the computer, we will schedule training sessions.

Answers and Explanations

1. B. Because this wish can't be fulfilled, the subjunctive verb form *were* is correct.

2. A. Since the president is optimistic, he believes revenues will increase. Therefore, use the indicative verb form *increase*.

3. A. The manager is not in the president's position, so the statement is contrary to fact, and the subjunctive form *were* is needed.

4. B. The president thinks it improbable that prices would rise, so the sentence uses the subjunctive *were*. If he believed prices would rise, choice A would be correct.

5. B. A stockholders' meeting is a formal situation, so the sentence requires a subjunctive verb: *were correct*.

6. A conversation during a golf game is an informal situation; the subjunctive form would seem pretentious. *Was right* is appropriate in this situation.

7. B. Since it isn't the manager's decision, a condition contrary to fact exists, requiring the subjunctive *were*.

8. A. This is a simple conditional statement, neither a wish nor contrary to fact. The subjunctive form is unnecessary. Additionally, choice B uses the subjunctive in the first clause and the indicative in the second clause, creating an awkward shift.

9. A. The simpler and more direct active voice is appropriate. The meaning does not require a passive construction.

10. B. The emphasis is on what the company plans to do—*we will schedule*. Use the active voice.

6
MODIFIERS

Why are modifiers important? For one thing, they form a part of almost every sentence we write. Important though the subject and the verb are few sentences consist solely of these words. The sentence "Honesty pays" illustrates the sentence that has only a subject and a verb, but such a sentence is quite unusual.

Even a simple sentence like, "The sales manager submitted a monthly report" contains four modifiers—*the* and *a* as articles, *sales* modifying manager and *monthly* modifying report. The more complex the thought becomes, the more relationships are shown between the ideas it contains, the more modifiers you must use. Modifiers are important, then, because they are a part of virtually every sentence we write.

Modifiers are important, too, because of the function they perform. They *describe, restrict, limit,* and *make more exact* the meaning of other words. You must then use your judgment in deciding *when* to use modifiers and in choosing the "precise" modifier to get your meaning across. In addition, if you are to write effectively you must be discriminating in your use of modifiers. You should not use too many for this will result in "wordy" sentences. Train yourself to shorten clause modifiers to phrases and phrases to single words whenever that is possible. And, finally, use modifiers with discretion, or they will change the "tone" of your writing. In letters, it is often the modifier that may unwittingly offend the reader; in reports, it is often the modifier that tends to destroy the objective, impartial tone of the exposition. Look at this example:

> The studio's president stated that he did not agree with the agent's requests.

The studio's president stated *flatly* that he did not agree with the agent's requests.

In the first example we have a simple statement of fact, objective and disinterested. In the second example, by adding one modifier (flatly) we have changed the tone of the sentence and injected a personal and biased note.

What, then, should you know about modifiers if you are to choose them wisely and use them effectively? Essentially, you must know:

(1) that in choosing modifiers—

    (a) you may use a single word, a phrase, or a clause

    (b) you may modify a subject, a verb, a complement, or another modifier

    (c) you must use adjective modifiers (whether words, phrases, or clauses) to modify subjects, objects, and predicate nominatives

    (d) you must use adverbial modifiers to modify verbs, adjectives, and other adverbs

(2) that in using modifiers—

    (a) you must place them as close as possible to the word(s) being modified

    (b) you must not misuse modifiers or you will confuse the reader

    (c) you must not overuse modifiers or you will ruin the conciseness of the writing

This chapter will explain and illustrate these and other related points and will demonstrate the more serious problems you might face in applying the principles governing modifiers.

Classification of Modifiers

Modifiers fall generally into two categories: *adjectives* and phrases or clauses used as adjectives; *adverbs* and phrases or clauses used as adverbs. Sometimes the form of the modifier clearly shows whether it is an adjective or an adverb; sometimes the form is the same for both.

Adjectives describe, limit, or make more exact the meaning of a noun or pronoun (any substantive).

Adverbs describe, limit, or make more exact the meaning of a verb, an adjective, or another adverb.

Types of Adjectives

There are six main categories of adjectives:

LIMITING:	*many* people, *much* work
NUMERICAL:	*four* letters, *nine* regions
DESCRIPTIVE:	*accurate* description, *long-term* project
PROPER:	*American* flag, *British* embassy
PRONOMINAL:	*my* assignment, *this* book
ARTICLE:	*a* letter, *an* hour, *the* return

Articles

The articles are *a*, *an*, and *the*. Use *a* before words beginning with a consonant sound, *an* before those beginning with a vowel sound.

a desk, *a* book

an error, *an* army

The article used before each of two connected nouns or adjectives signals that the words refer to different people or things.

We elected *a* secretary and *a* treasurer (two persons).

She owns *a* black and silver automobile (one car, two colors).

Do not use *a* or *an* after *sort of, kind of, manner of, style of,* or *type of.*

NOT: What *kind of a* book do you want?
BUT: What *kind of* book do you want?

Types of Adverbs

Adverbs may be classified according to the questions they answer; in general, there are five types:

Adverbs of manner:	run *swiftly*, write *legibly*, compute *accurately*
Adverbs of place and direction:	*above, before, below, here, out*
Adverbs of time and succession:	*immediately, today, ago, lately*
Adverbs of degree and measure:	*almost, enough, far, little, much*

Adverbs of cause, reason, or purpose: because, hence, therefore

Identifying Adjectives and Adverbs

Sometimes it is difficult to distinguish between adjectives and adverbs. Here are a few illustrative examples.

The -*ly* Ending

Some adverbs, primarily the adverbs of manner, are formed by adding -*ly* to the adjective or participle form. However, not all adverbs end in -*ly;* and some adjectives end in -*ly*. The writer cannot, then, look upon the -*ly* ending as a means of distinguishing between adjectives and adverbs.

Adjectives that End in -ly:

cleanly, deadly, friendly, likely, lively, lonely, lovely, kindly, orderly, timely

a *friendly* discussion, an *orderly* arrangement, a *timely* return.

Adverbs that Do Not End in -ly:

soon, often, around, down, very, now, yet
write *soon*, call *often*, *very* high production

Words That Are Both Adjectives and Adverbs

The following words may be either adjectives or adverbs, depending on their use:

> above, bad, better, cheap, close, deep, early, fast, first, hard, late, long, loud, much, only, quick, slow, very, well

> Henry types *better* than Andy does. (adverb)
> The teacher had a cold, but she is *better* now. (adjective)

> We climbed *very* rapidly. (adverb)
> That is the *very* report I was looking for. (adjective)

> If you must use the detour, drive *slow* (or slowly). (adverb)
> A *slow* driver is often a hazard on the highway. (adjective)

Adverbs with Two Forms

Some adverbs have two forms—one ending in -*ly*, the other not. The longer form is nearly always correct and is preferable in formal writing. The short form is properly used in brief, forceful sentences (in commands—such as the road sign *Drive Slow*) and may be used in informal writing. The -*ly* form should, however, always be used to modify an adjective.

Following are examples of adverbs having two forms:

slow, slowly	clear, clearly	quick, quickly
cheap, cheaply	sharp, sharply	loud, loudly
soft, softly	deep, deeply	direct, directly

Sometimes the meaning desired will determine which form should be used. Notice that either *direct* or *directly* may be used when the meaning is "in a straight line," but *directly* is the only choice when *soon* is meant.

In informal speech, we sometimes drop the -*ly* ending from some often-used adverbs. This practice is incorrect and, even though we occasionally let it slip by in our speech, we must not allow it in our writing.

Correct Usage

> I am *really* glad you could come.   (NOT: *real* glad)
>
> I'm feeling *considerably* better.   (NOT: *considerable)*
>
> Elvis *surely* is lucky.   (NOT: *sure)*

Distinguishing Between a Predicate Adjective and an Adverb

A predicate adjective is, as its name implies, an adjective appearing in the predicate and modifying the subject. The following categories of verbs (called *linking verbs)* are usually followed by a predicate adjective rather than by an adverb. A predicate adjective can occur only after these verbs:

(1) Forms of the verb *to be*
    That man is *old.* (old man)
    The report was *accurate.* (accurate report)

(2) Other no-action verbs, such as *become, appear, seem*
    The town appears *deserted.* (deserted town)
    The air seems *humid.* (humid air)

(3) Verbs pertaining to the senses
    The reports sound *exaggerated.* (exaggerated reports)
    The peach tastes *sweet.* (sweet peach)
    The work looks *hard.* (hard work)

Be sure to distinguish between the predicate adjective and the adverb when the sense verbs are used. Usually these verbs are followed by adjectives, but they may be modified by adverbs.

> She looks *bad.* (She doesn't appear to be healthy.)
>
> She looks *badly.* (An awkward construction, which could mean that, having lost something, she is doing a poor job of looking for it.)
>
> The steak looks *tender.* (has the appearance of *tender* steak)
>
> The woman looked *tenderly* at the child. (tells "how" she *looked* at the child)

The child looks *wistful*. (has a wistful look)

The child looked *wistfully* at the candy. (tells how the child *looked* at the candy)

To determine whether the modifier following a sense verb modifies the subject or the verb, substitute *is* or *are* for the sense verb. If, after this substitution, the sentence is logical, you can be sure your choice (whether of a predicate adjective or an adverb) is correct.

The steak is *tender*. (logical)

The woman is *tenderly* at the child. (illogical)

Compound Modifiers (With and Without Hyphens)

Modifiers Preceding a Noun

Two or more words serving as a single adjective are called a compound adjective. When these modifiers *precede* a noun, they are joined by a hyphen.

Have you an *up-to-date report* on that subject?

Please submit the *above-mentioned form* in duplicate.

That is a *well-written story*.

Ours is a *well-equipped school*.

Modifiers Following a Noun

When the modifying words *follow* a noun, do not use a hyphen unless the words are listed as hyphenated compounds in the dictionary.

This *report* is *up to date*.

The *form mentioned above* must be submitted in duplicate.

That *story* is *well written*.

Our *school* is *well equipped*.

This word processing program is *self-starting*.

Since usage is constantly changing, it is best to consult a recent dictionary when in doubt about hyphenated words. Notice that, in the last example above, *self-starting* is hyphenated, even though it follows the noun. The dictionary gives all "self'" words except *self-same, selfish, selfhood,* and *selfless* as hyphenated compounds.

Suspending Hyphens

In a series of hyphenated adjective-noun words having a common ending, suspending hyphens are used to carry the force of the modifier over to a later noun.

Is he looking for a two- or three-bedroom apartment?

It is a 4- or 5-page report.

Two-Word Proper Adjectives

Compound adjectives consisting of two-word proper adjectives are *not* hyphenated.

He is vacationing at a *New Jersey* beach.

Separate Modifiers Preceding a Noun

Do not hyphenate two or more adjectives that precede the noun *if they do not act jointly to modify the noun.* Note, however, the correct punctuation of such a construction.

He wore a *white flannel suit.* (a flannel suit that was white)

Give me a *current statistical report.* (a statistical report that is current)

It was a *long, hard job.* (a long job and a hard one)

It was an *involved, difficult case.* (an involved case and a difficult one)

One way to help determine whether to put a comma between the two adjectives is that if you can insert the word *and* between the two adjectives without destroying the meaning of the sentence, use a comma; otherwise, do not.

Adverb Ending in -*ly* with Adjective

Do not use a hyphen between an adverb ending in -*ly* and an adjective or participle.

This is a *carefully written story.*

That is a *frequently quoted passage.*

Comparison of Adjectives and Adverbs

Degrees of Comparison

Adjectives and adverbs change form to show a greater or lesser degree of the characteristic named by the simple word. There are three degrees of comparison.

Positive degree—The positive degree names the *quality* expressed by the adjective or adverb. It does not imply a comparison with, or a relation to, a similar quality in any other thing.

high morale, a *dependable* player, work *fast*, prepared *carefully*

Comparative degree—The comparative degree indicates that the quality described by the modifier exists to a greater or lesser degree in one thing than in another. It is formed by adding -*er* to the positive degree or by inserting *more* or *less* before the positive form.

Our organization has *higher* morale now than ever before.

She is a *more dependable* player than Teresa.

She can work *faster* than I.

This report was prepared *more carefully* than the one submitted last month.

Superlative degree—The superlative degree denotes the greatest or least amount of the quality named. It is formed by adding -*est* to the positive degree of the adjective or adverb or by inserting *most* or *least* before the positive form.

That organization has the *highest* morale of any in this city.

She is the *most dependable* player on the team.

This is the *most carefully* prepared report I have found.

The comparative degree is used to refer to only two things, the superlative to more than two.

This book is the *longer* of the two.

This book is the *longest* of the three.

Using -*Er* and -*Est* vs. *More* and *Most*

There is no difference in meaning between -*er* and *more* or between -*est* and *most*. Either method may be used with some modifiers. However, most adjectives of three syllables or more and almost all adverbs are compared by the use of *more* and *most* (or *less* and *least*) rather than by the endings -*er* and -*est*. In choosing which method should be used with the modifiers that may take either method, you may base your choice on emphasis. By adding -*er* or -*est* to the root word you emphasize the *quality*, while by using *more* or *most* you stress the *degree* of comparison.

Should I have been *kinder* or *harsher* in handling her problem?

That story is the *longest* of the three.

Should I have been *more firm* or *less firm* in handling her problem?

Of all the forms, this one is the *most simple* and that one is the *least simple* to fill out.

While either -*er* or *more* can be used for the comparative, and -*est* or *most* can be used for the superlative, be sure not to use both the suffix and the adverb.

NOT: That solution to the problem is *more simpler* than this one.

BUT: That solution to the problem is *simpler* than this one.

OR: That solution to the problem is *more simple* than this one.

NOT: Wetso Soap keeps your hands *most cleanest.*
BUT: Wetso Soap keeps your hands *cleanest.*
OR: Wetso Soap keeps your hands *most clean.*

Irregular Comparisons

Some modifiers are compared by changes in the words themselves. A few of these irregular comparisons are given below; consult your dictionary whenever you are in doubt about the comparison of any adjective or adverb.

Positive	Comparative	Superlative
good	better	best
well	better	best
bad (evil, ill)	worse	worst
badly (ill)	worse	worst
far	farther, further	farthest, furthest
late	later, latter	latest, last
little	less, lesser	least
many, much	more	most

Problems with Comparison

Some adjectives and adverbs express qualities that cannot be used in comparisons. They represent the highest degree of a quality and, as a result, cannot be improved. Some of these words are listed below:

complete	infinitely	square
correct	perfect	squarely
dead	perfectly	supreme
deadly	perpendicularly	totally
exact	preferable	unique
horizontally	round	uniquely
immortally	secondly	universally

However, there may be times when the comparison of these words is justified. If we use these modifiers in a relative or approximate sense, they may be compared. But proceed with care. It is usually better, for example, to say *more nearly round* or *more nearly perfect* than *rounder* or *more perfect.*

Incomplete Comparison

When you make a comparison between two items, be sure that both terms of the comparison are named. If you don't, the reader may not understand which of two items you are comparing. Be sure your reader knows exactly what you mean when you say:

> There have been more successful prosecutions of robbery cases in the city this year. (Do you mean *more than in any other city* or *more than in any previous year?*)

Whenever a comparison is not completed, the meaning of the sentence is obscured. This is one form of the incomplete comparison. Here are a few more.

(1) Incomplete comparison—with possessive:

OBSCURE:	Joan's letter states the problem better than John. (We cannot tell whether it is *John* or *John's letter* that is stating the problem.)
IMPROVED:	Joan's letter states the problem better than John's.

(2) Incomplete comparison—with conjunction:

OBSCURE:	This text is as good, if not better than that one. (Because of the omission of the second *as* after *good*, this sentence reads—as *good than*.)
IMPROVED:	This text is as good *as*, if not better than, that one.
OR:	This text is as good as that one, if not better.
OBSCURE:	This book is shorter, but just as comprehensive as that one.
IMPROVED:	This book is shorter *than*, but just as comprehensive as, that one.
OR:	This book is shorter than that one, but just as comprehensive.

(3) Incomplete comparison—with verb:

AMBIGUOUS:	I enjoy this kind of work more than Andrew. (This could be interpreted—I enjoy this kind of work more than I enjoy *Andrew*.)
IMPROVED:	I enjoy this kind of work more than Andrew *does*.

OBSCURE: I have known her longer than Melinda.

COULD MEAN: I have known her longer than Melinda *has*.

OR: I have known her longer than *I have known* Melinda.

Verbals and Verbal Phrases as Modifiers

Verbals, words derived from verbs, are sometimes used as modifiers, either singly or in phrases.

Infinitive

The infinitive may serve either as an adjective or as an adverb. And, as a modifier, it may be used either with or without the introductory *to*.

As an *adjective:*

We heard *him speak.* (heard him (to) speak)

The *essay to be revised* is on my desk.

As an *adverb*:

I am *ready to write* the letter now.

I am *unable to speak* on that subject.

We will *try to finish* before noon.

The manager *wrote* this letter *to explain* our service policy.

Much has been written on whether it is good usage to split an infinitive—that is, whether to insert a modifying word between the *to* and the rest of the infinitive *(to carefully consider* instead of *to consider carefully)*. The problem most often arises when a modified infinitive follows another verb construction.

Take, for example, the problem you face in inserting the adverb *completely* in this sentence, "He wished to forget the controversy with his staff."

Placed before the infinitive—"He wished *completely to forget* the controversy with his staff"—*completely* becomes a squinting modifier;

it could modify either the infinitive or the verb *wished*.

Placed after the infinitive—"He wished *to forget* the controversy *completely* with his staff"—*completely* loses most of its force because it is so far removed from the infinitive it is modifying.

Now, let's split the infinitive—"He wished *to completely forget* the controversy with his staff." Despite the split infinitive, this construction seems the smoothest and most desirable of the three.

As you can see from this illustration, it may be unwise to make the flat statement that an infinitive must *never* be split. Most grammarians recommend that writers avoid splitting an infinitive whenever possible (even if recasting the sentence is necessary), but they endorse the split infinitive if avoiding it would result in an awkward or ambiguous sentence.

Infinitive Phrase

An infinitive phrase (an infinitive plus the words modifying it or completing it) may also be used as a modifier.

To get the most out of this course, you must study regularly.

To complete the report on time, the class should start gathering data now.

Participle

The participle, in all three forms (present, past, and perfect) is an adjective.

PRESENT PARTICIPLE:	ends in *-ing*, as *talking, building, writing*
PAST PARTICIPLE:	verb form usually ending in *-ed*, sometimes in *-t*, and sometimes an irregular ending: *forgotten, borne, written*
PERFECT PARTICIPLE:	verb form consisting of *having* or *having been* plus the past participle, as *having talked, having built, having written, having been written*

Rising, the president greeted the caller. (*Rising* is a present participle modifying president.)

The *letter, typed* and *signed,* was mailed. (*Typed* and *signed* are past participles modifying letter.)

The *letter, having been corrected,* was ready for signature. (*Having been corrected* is a perfect participle modifying letter.)

Participial Phrase

A participial phrase (a participle combined with its object or modifying words) functions as an adjective.

Leaving his desk, the *clerk* opened the file cabinet.

Putting on her coat, she prepared to leave the office.

The *draft, composed hurriedly,* was on her desk.

The *fax, sent in error,* could not be recovered.

The *coach, having called the meeting for 2 o'clock,* was waiting in her office.

The *meeting, having been called for 2 o'clock,* had to be postponed.

Gerund Phrase

The gerund phrase (composed of a gerund plus its subject, complement, or modifier), like the gerund itself, serves as a noun. But when this phrase becomes the object of a preposition, the resulting prepositional-gerund phrase may serve as an *adjective* or as an *adverb.* It is this use of the gerund phrase with which we are concerned.

After meeting with representatives of the employee group, she announced her decision.

In making our decision, we carefully considered both sides of the question.

He *ended* his report *by summarizing his conclusions.* (serves as adverb; phrase modifies *ended*)

Dangling Verbal Phrases

The term *dangling* is quite descriptive of what happens when an infinitive, participial, or prepositional—gerund phrase cannot refer, both logically and grammatically, to a noun or pronoun serving as the subject of the main clause of a sentence.

Since such phrases are said to *attach* to the subject of the main clause, it is easy to see that they can only *dangle* until you take corrective action. This you can do in either of two ways: (1) by changing the subject of the main clause to one which the phrase may refer to, or (2) by changing the phrase itself into a dependent clause, so that it has a subject of its own.

(1) DANGLING: *To get the most out of this course,* careful *study is* necessary. (The phrase cannot logically modify *study;* so it dangles.)

CORRECTED: *To get the most out of this course, you* must study it carefully.

(2) DANGLING: *To apply for this job, a Form 57* must be completed. (A *form* can't apply for a job; consequently, the phrase dangles.)

CORRECTED: *To apply for this job,* the *applicant* must complete a Form 57.

OR: When the *applicant* applies for the job, a Form 57 must be completed.

(3) DANGLING: *Rushing to meet the deadline for the project,* many *errors* were made. (Dangles: It wasn't the *errors* that were rushing to meet the deadline.)

CORRECTED: *Rushing to meet the deadline for the project, they* made many errors.

OR: Because *they* rushed to meet the deadline for the project, many errors were made.

An infinitive or a participial phrase that modifies the whole sentence, designating general action rather than action by a specific element, may be correctly used without relation to the subject of the main clause.

Generally speaking, these plants grow better in sunlight.

To summarize, the plan should be ready to put into effect next fall.

Nominative Absolute—the Sentence Modifier

The *nominative absolute*, or simple *absolute*, modifies the whole sentence rather than a specific element in it. Unlike the participial phrase which it resembles, *the absolute has its own subject*. It therefore is grammatically independent of the rest of the sentence and does not dangle when it does not refer to the subject of the main clause.

All things considered, you have done a fine job. *(Things* is the subject of the absolute phrase.)

The *game being over*, we went home.

Clear *weather having been forecast*, we completed our plans for the office picnic.

The *supervisor having left the office*, the assistant took the call.

Prepositional Phrase as a Modifier

The prepositional phrase—composed of the preposition, its object, and any modifiers of the object—may serve as an adjective or as an adverb.

As an adjective:

The letter was addressed to the *office of the principal*. (*of the principal* modifies *office*.)

I hope we don't have another *conference like the one we had yesterday*. (Phrase modifies *conference*. *Like* is the preposition; *one* is its object; and the clause *(that) we had yesterday* modifies *one*.)

As an adverb:

They *have gone to the movies*. (*to the movies* modifies the verb *have gone*.)

Give it *to the person who answers the door*. (The phrase modifies the verb *give.* Within the phrase, *to* is the preposition; *person* is its object; the clause *who answers the door* modifies the object.)

Dangling Prepositional Phrase

A prepositional phrase *dangles* when it does not, both logically and grammatically, refer to the subject of the main clause.

> DANGLING: *With much effort,* the *report* was completed on time.
>
> CORRECTED: *With much effort, we* completed the report on time.

Dependent Clauses as Modifiers

Dependent clauses may serve as adjectives or as adverbs. The words that introduce them play a dual role—connecting (or linking) the clause with the rest of the sentence and showing the relationship between the dependent clause and the rest of the sentence.

Dependent Clauses as Adjectives

Dependent clauses that serve as adjectives may be introduced by either relative pronouns (that, which, who, whom, whatever, whichever, whoever, whomever) or relative adverbs (where, when, while).

By *relative pronouns*—

> The *memorandum that is on your desk* has been revised.
>
> The *client who called for an appointment* is here.
>
> Your *letter* of May 25, *which called our attention to the error,* was answered yesterday.

By *relative adverbs*—

> This is the *building where our office is located.*
>
> We caught him at a *time when he was not busy.*

Note: An adjective clause may be restrictive or nonrestrictive.

Restrictive clauses cannot be omitted without changing the meaning of the sentence. They restrict or limit the word preceding them, and by answering the question, "Which one?" they also serve an identifying function. Because they are an essential part of the sentence, they are not set off by commas.

Nonrestrictive clauses, on the other hand, are not essential to the meaning of the sentence. They may add interesting or helpful information, but they are not necessary as restrictive clauses are. To show that they contain ideas of secondary importance, nonrestrictive clauses are set off by commas.

> The person *who is sitting at the front desk* is the receptionist. (Restrictive clause. Essential to meaning of sentence, it answers the question *Which one?*)

> Terry, *who is sitting at the front desk,* is the receptionist. (Nonrestrictive clause. It adds another thought, but it is not essential to the meaning of the sentence.)

Dependent Clauses as Adverbs

Dependent clauses that serve as adverbs are introduced by subordinating conjunctions. A few of these conjunctions are: as, because, since, although, if, provided, after.

> *While we were reviewing the report,* we *noticed* several errors in sentence construction.

> *Before we approved the report,* we *inserted* a qualifying statement.

Elliptical Clauses

Parts of a dependent clause are sometimes omitted because the writer feels that the reader can easily supply the missing elements. These incomplete clauses are known as *elliptical clauses.* An elliptical clause must be able to modify, both logically and grammatically, the subject of the main clause. If it does not, it dangles.

To correct a dangling elliptical clause we may either (1) change the subject of the main clause to one which the elliptical clause can logically modify or (2) supply the missing elements in the elliptical clause.

DANGLING: *Unless compiled by early June,* we cannot include the figures in this year's annual report.

CORRECTED: *Unless compiled by early June,* the figures cannot be included in this year's annual report.

OR: Unless *the figures are* compiled by early June, we cannot include them in this year's annual report.

DANGLING: *While making a periodic tour of the factory,* a few changes in procedure were recommended.

CORRECTED: *While making a periodic tour of the factory, the engineer* recommended a few changes in procedure.

OR: While *the engineer was* making a periodic tour of the factory, a few changes in procedure were recommended.

Relative Pronouns Introducing Clauses

Be careful to select the correct relative pronoun to introduce the adjective clause. *Who* refers to *persons; which* refers to *things; that* usually refers to *things* but is sometimes used to refer to *persons.*

The *investigator who submitted this report* has had extensive experience.

The monthly *report, which is due tomorrow,* will contain that information.

The statistical *report that you have been submitting weekly* will be required once a month from now on.

Which may introduce either a restrictive or a nonrestrictive clause. *That* introduces restrictive clauses only.

The assignment *that* (or *which) the student is working on* is a particularly complicated one. (The restrictive clause is necessary to identify the assignment.)

The history class *assignment, which* the student *is working on,* is a particularly complicated one. (Nonrestrictive clause. The assignment is already identified by name.)

The report *that* (or *which) is on my desk* is ready to be sent. (Restrictive clause.)

The monthly statistical *report, which is on my desk,* is ready to be sent. (Nonrestrictive clause. It is not essential to meaning.)

We may use *that* in place of *who* to refer to persons if we mean a *class or type of person* rather than an individual.

Any salesperson *that works in the general office of the company* is eligible to attend this program. (Refers to a class or type of employee.)

The attorney *who sits at that desk* is Ms. Monahan. (Refers to a specific individual.)

Whose may be used as the possessive of any of these relative pronouns—who, which, that.

The cook *whose job was abolished* has been reassigned.

This is the book *whose approach has been the subject of so much discussion.* (This use of *whose* to refer to inanimate objects is acceptable in informal speaking and writing; the phrase *of which* is preferred in formal writing.)

Placement of Modifiers

High on the list of sentence errors is the *misplaced modifier.*

Modifiers should be placed as close as possible to the words they modify. This is true whether the modifier is a single word, a phrase, or a clause. In English, the only way the reader can tell which word is being modified is by the location of the modifier. Meaning is simply a matter of geography.

Many ambiguous (and unintentionally humorous) sentences result from the misplacement of modifiers.

Modifier Between Subject and Verb

Wherever possible, avoid placing the modifier between subject and verb and between verb and object.

NOT: The accountant, *to explain the difference between gross income and net income,* used several illustrations.

BUT: *To explain the difference between gross income and net income,* the accountant used several illustrations.

OR: The accountant used several illustrations *to explain the difference between gross income and net income.*

Single Adjectives

A single adjective is usually placed immediately *before* the word it modifies.

NOT: I would like *a cold* glass of water.

BUT: I would like a glass of *cold* water. (It is the water, not the glass, that should be cold)

Multiple Adjectives

To make sure their sentences read more smoothly, writers may also place immediately after the word—

(1) A modifier consisting of two or more adjectives. (The report—*long, tedious,* and *involved*—was finally completed.)

(2) A modifier consisting of one or more adverbs plus an adjective. (The report—*carefully written* and *well documented*—was submitted to the committee.)

Single Adverbs

Some adverbs—only, almost, nearly, also, quite, merely, actually—are frequent troublemakers. Be sure they are placed as close as possible to the words they modify.

EXAMPLE: The problem can *only* be answered by the teacher.

COULD MEAN: *Only* the teacher can answer the problem.

OR: The teacher can *only* answer the problem, not explain it.

Phrases and Clauses

Phrases and clauses, like single-word modifiers, should be placed as close as possible to the words they modify, so there will be no danger of their attaching themselves to the wrong sentence element.

NOT: We need someone to write programs *with statistical experience.* (the programs do not have experience)

BUT: We need *someone with statistical experience* to write programs.

NOT: Mr. Dough has resigned from the presidency of the club after *having served* four years *to the regret of all the members.* (The sentence means they regretted his four years of service)

BUT: *To the regret of all the members,* Mr. Dough *has resigned* from the presidency of the club after having served four years.

Relative Clauses

Relative clauses should also be placed immediately after the word they modify, since they attach themselves to the sentence element nearest them.

NOT: The *writer* has an *appointment that is waiting in my office.* (the appointment is waiting)

BUT: The *writer that is waiting in my office* has an appointment.

Squinting Constructions

Avoid *squinting constructions*—that is, modifiers that are placed so that the reader cannot tell whether they are modifying the words immediately preceding them or those immediately following them.

OBSCURE: The lawyer *agreed after the papers were signed to take* the case.

COULD MEAN: The lawyer agreed *to take* the case *after the papers were signed.*

OR: *After the papers were signed,* the lawyer *agreed* to take the case.

Adverb Clauses

An adverb clause may be placed either at the beginning of a sentence or, in its natural order, after the main clause. There are two reasons why we might choose to place the adverb clause first: (1) to put greater emphasis on the main clause; (2) to avoid piling up modifying clauses after the main clause. (An introductory adverb clause—sometimes called an *inverted clause* since it is out of its natural order—should usually be followed by a comma.)

NATURAL ORDER: This report must contain information from all the schools in the region *if it is to reflect a true picture of our activities.*

INVERTED ORDER: *If the report is to reflect a true picture of our activities,* it must contain information from all the schools in the region. (More emphatic)

Long Modifying Phrases

A long or complex modifying phrase at the end of the sentence has an anticlimactic effect. We strengthen our writing when we place such phrases before the main clause.

WEAK: We have asked each department to tell us the number of copies it will need *in order to ensure adequate distribution of this report.*

STRONGER: *In order to ensure adequate distribution of this report,* we have asked each department to tell us the number of copies it will need.

WEAK: We will send two examination copies of the book to each reviewer *immediately after its completion.*

STRONGER: *Immediately after the book is completed,* we will send two examination copies to each reviewer.

Quiz

To review your understanding of how modifiers contribute to meaning, practice with the following quiz.

Directions: Each item presents two sentences. Choose the sentence which more clearly conveys its meaning by using modifiers correctly.

1. A. Comedies are the type of a film I enjoy most.

   B. Comedies are the type of film I enjoy most.

2. A. I happy pay the admission price to see those films.

   B. I happily pay the admission price to see those films.

3. A. The early showing begins at 6:00 P.M.

   B. The lately showing begins at 10:30 P.M.

4. A. I was real pleased to hear about your promotion.

   B. I was really pleased to hear about your promotion.

5. A. Taxes in California are among the higher of all the states.

   B. Taxes in California are among the highest of all the states.

6. A. Missouri has a more lower tax rate.

   B. Missouri has a lower tax rate.

7. A. Form 1040-E is the most easy to complete.

   B. Form 1040-E is the easiest to complete.

8. A. In this case, the accountant enjoyed his work more than the attorney did.

   B. In this case, the accountant enjoyed his work more than the attorney.

9. A. The show opened with a voice saying the mission was to boldly go to places never visited before.

   B. The show opened with a voice saying the mission was to go boldly to places never visited before.

10. A. Upon seeing the planet, the commander of the ship slowed the warp drive.

    B. Upon seeing the planet, the ship slowed the warp drive.

11. A. The commander only has the authority to do this.

    B. Only the commander has the authority to do this.

12. A. The crew left the planet, where they had been on leave in a shuttle craft.

    B. Flying in a shuttle craft, the crew left the planet where they had been on leave.

Answers and Explanations

1. B. Do not use *a* after *sort of, kind of, manner of, style of,* or *type of.*

2. B. Use an adverb, *happily,* not an adjective, *happy,* to modify the verb *pay.*

3. A. The adjective modifying *showing* is *early. Lately* is an adverb.

4. B. Although heard in informal speech, the use of *real* or *sure* to modify the adjective *pleased* is incorrect in standard written English.

5. B. Use the superlative form to compare more than two items. The word *among* indicates more than two items are compared.

6. B. Do not use both *more* and *-er* to express the comparative.

7. B. Do not use both *most* and *-est* to express the superlative.

8. A. Choice B could mean the accountant enjoyed his work more than the attorney enjoyed the work, or it could mean the accountant enjoyed his work more than he enjoyed working with the attorney. To revise a dangling elliptical clause, add the missing element in the clause, the verb *did*.

9. A. Although this choice splits the infinitive, *to boldly go* sounds smoother than *to go boldly*. *To go boldly* creates a rhyme between *go* and *bo*—which makes the phrase sound silly. (Note: Some readers may recognize this phrase as part of the opening of the television series *Star Trek*.)

10. A. In choice B, the ship sees the planet. Technology may produce wonders, but ships that literally see is an inaccurate personification. To avoid dangling prepositional phrases (*upon seeing the planet*), change the subject of the main clause from *ship* to *the commander of the ship*.

11. B. Is the commander the only person who has the authority to do this, or is this the sole authority the commander has? Logic suggests the former. A commander would have more than one area to supervise. Place adverbs as close as possible to the words they modify.

12. B. Choice A suggests they had spent their leave in a craft designed to fly from place to place. Place modifying phrases next to the word or phrase they modify.

7
CONNECTIVES

You have probably noticed that young children speak in short sentences one after another, with no connectives to show the relationships between the sentences. As we grow older, we want to communicate more complex thoughts. Connectives provide a means of showing relationships between ideas. They clarify meaning.

Our language is filled with connectives. We can be selective in choosing the one that will express our meaning exactly. By our *choice* of connectives, we can clarify the precise relationship between two ideas. By our *use* of connectives, we can guide the reader from the beginning of our writing through to the end—signaling along the way when we are going to add a thought, change to a different point of view, or shift to a different subject.

Connectives are to writing what directional signals are to driving. Just as a flashing signal alerts the driver of the car behind that we are going to turn right, so a well-chosen connective signals the reader that we are going to change our approach. Confusion (or worse) results when the driver either fails to signal or signals incorrectly. Likewise, confusion results when the writer fails to signal the reader or signals incorrectly. One more similarity—as drivers, we sometimes become indignant with the driver in front when he fails to signal, even though we ourselves may not be signaling the driver behind us. As readers, we often rely heavily on the connectives which the writer has used, even though we may not, as writers, be equally concerned about signaling to our readers.

Connectives, then, are important signals which both writers and readers should be familiar with. They should be used skillfully as an effective means of transferring thought from one mind to another.

Four kinds of words can serve as connectives—prepositions, conjunctions, relative pronouns, and relative adverbs. Each not only connects two sentence elements but also shows the relationship between them.

Prepositions

A preposition *connects* the word, phrase, or clause that follows it (its object) with some other element in the sentence *and shows the relationship* between them.

There are three kinds of prepositions:

Simple prepositions

at	but	by	down	for
from	in	like	of	off
on	out	over	per	through
till	to	up	via	with

Compound prepositions

about	above	across	after	against
along	among	around	before	behind
below	beneath	beside	besides	between
beyond	despite	except	inside	into
outside	toward(s)	under	until	upon
within	without			

Phrasal prepositions (two or more words that function as a single preposition)

according to	contrary to
because of	inasmuch as

Choice of Preposition

Choosing the preposition is usually either no problem at all for the writer or a problem that seems to defy a reasonable solution.

When the choice is simple, it is because prepositions have become such a basic part of our vocabularies that we choose them almost without being aware of making a choice. In many constructions, one preposition just seems right; another, wrong.

When the choice is difficult, it is because we lack this sensing of the essential rightness or wrongness of the preposition. When we are unable to select the appropriate preposition, we look for a rule of grammar to help us make a choice. Then we find that there *is* no governing rule of grammar; idiomatic usage is the only key.

Idioms and Idiomatic Usage

In English, as in other languages, there has developed over the years a set of language patterns that we call grammar. Within this structure, a body of formal rules may be found side by side with a body of informal exceptions to those rules. These "exceptions" reflect traditions of speech and represent popular and accepted usage.

Idiom is often quite different from grammar and often conflicts with it. When we say that something is *idiomatic usage,* we mean that everyday usage has established it as correct and acceptable, whether or not it conflicts with grammar.

It is idiom that requires us to say—

able *to* work	but	capable *of* working
the way *to* cut	but	the way *of* cutting (method)
aim *at* getting	but	try *to* get

Grammar doesn't help us to make this choice. For, as far as grammar is concerned, in each of the three illustrations, *to, of, for,* and *at* are equally acceptable. But idiom says, "It doesn't *make sense* to say *aim to getting;* only *aim at getting* can get the idea across."

Fortunately, if English is our native language, most of these idiomatic expressions are so ingrained that we use them instinctively and cringe when we hear them misused. However, when we cannot make this instinctive choice, we must make it our business to find out what the idiomatic usage is.

Choice Based on Shades of Meaning

The choice between prepositions is often based on the slight difference in meaning between them or on the preference which grammarians have expressed.

At, In

These two prepositions often may be used interchangeably. However, when they are used in phrases giving the place or locality of an action, writers should be aware of these distinctions:

(1) *In* is used when reference to the interior of a building is stressed; *At*, when the site itself is stressed.
We held our conference *in* the City Auditorium.
We arranged to meet *at* the City Auditorium.

(2) *In* is usually used before the names of countries, states, cities, and sections; *At*, before the names of business firms, office buildings, and so on.
In France; *In* the North; *In* the Southwest
At the post office; *At* Blank and Company
At Yale. (Clinton was educated *at* Yale.)

(3) *In* is used before the name of a city if the writer wants to leave an impression of permanence; *At*, if he wants to indicate a temporary stay.
Following a brief stopover *at* Chicago, we spent 2 weeks *in* Minneapolis.
Johnson works *at* Dallas, but lives *in* Fort Worth.

(4) In local address *in* is used before the name of the city; *at*, before the street number of the residence or office.
Lincoln lives *at* 745 Main Street *in* Silver City.

Between, Among

Most of us know and apply the familiar rule: Use *among* when referring to more than two persons, things, or groups considered collectively; use *between* when referring to only two.

The estate was divided *among* the five heirs.

The property was divided *between* the city and the state.

We may not know, however, that *between* can and should be used in certain constructions in which more than two things are referred to. These are, of course, constructions that are somewhat unusual. Before we explain this further, consider these alternatives: Which would you say—

(1) A treaty *among* three nations (or *between three nations*)

(2) The contest is *among* the four candidates (or *between the four*)

(3) We must choose *among* the three plans (or *between the three plans*)

Perhaps you think that neither *between* nor *among* expresses the relationship clearly. But the fact is that there is no preposition in our language that can express the relation of a thing to several other things, not only with respect to its relation to the group as a whole but also with respect to its relation to each of the members as well.

Grammarians therefore agree that, in such constructions as those illustrated, *between* is a better and more logical choice than *among*.

Below, Beneath, Down, Under, Underneath

Sometimes the slight distinction in the use of prepositions concerns us, not because the use of one instead of another will *confuse* the readers but because it may *offend* them.

All five of the prepositions in this section may, in many cases, be used interchangeably. Even when they cannot, the choice is an easy one for us because the distinctions are so natural; for example, we say "his knees shook *beneath* him" but not "his knees shook *below* him." Grammatically, either is correct; idiom, however, makes the latter sound ridiculous.

But consider these distinctions:

The student says: "My sister is in the class *below* me."

Not: "My sister is in the class *beneath* me." (Here, *beneath* seems to imply inferiority or contempt.)

We say, quite properly, that someone is "*under* our care" or "*under* our supervision," but to say that someone is "*beneath* our care" or "*beneath* our notice" would be to speak contemptuously of him.

Here, too, our instinct usually guides us in using the word that will not offend, but courtesy, in both oral and written communication, requires us to be on the alert for any unintentional violation of this idiomatic usage.

Using the Single Instead of the Phrasal Preposition

One of the chief criticisms of phrasal prepositions is that they are somewhat wordy, often pompous, and hard to understand.

Here are only a few of the phrasal prepositions which should be replaced as often as possible with single prepositions that would make your writing less imposing and more concise:

NOT:	BUT:
inasmuch as	since
for the purpose of	to
prior to	before
subsequent to	after
in regard to	about

Inasmuch as the player has signed the contract ... *(Since)*

Unless we receive your payment *prior to* ... *(before)*

Subsequent to our conference with you ... *(After, since)*

We were asked to submit information *with regard to* available apartments. (about)

Placement of Preposition

The strong conviction that a sentence should not end with a preposition was, for a long time, shared by many people. However, this is not a rule.

There are at least three explanations for the growth of this conviction: (1) the rule of rhetoric that a sentence should end with a strong word—a noun, pronoun, verb, etc; (2) the nature of the word *preposition*—because of its prefix *pre* (meaning *before*), many believed that a preposition necessarily must *come before* another word; and (3) the illiterate use of an unnecessary preposition at the end of the sentence—"Where were you *at?*"

When one makes a studied effort to avoid ending a sentence with a preposition, it often results in a sentence that is unnatural, awkward, and sometimes confusing.

Consider these illustrations, which you will probably agree are much more natural than they would be if they were reconstructed to avoid the terminal preposition:

> What did you do that *for?*
>
> Here is the report that was sent *in*.
>
> We had many problems to talk *about*.
>
> Tell me what it is you object *to*.

Superfluous Prepositions

In talking, more than in writing, we tend to use double prepositions when only one is needed. We should take care lest this informal colloquial use creep into our writing.

> NOT: We will divide *up* the work.
> BUT: We will divide the work.

> NOT: The security guard is standing near *to* the door.
> BUT: The security guard is standing near the door.

> NOT: When are you going to start *in* to do the assignment?
> BUT: When are you going to start to do the assignment?

Faulty Omission of Prepositions

In formal writing, repeat the preposition before the second of two connected elements.

> NOT: The counselor seemed interested in us and our problems.
> BUT: The counselor seemed interested in us and *in* our problems.

> NOT: Sharon was able to complete the book report by planning carefully and working diligently.

BUT: Sharon was able to complete the book report by planning carefully and *by* working diligently.

In the so-called *split* (or *suspended*) *construction,* in which two words are completed by different prepositions, be especially careful to use both prepositions.

NOT: Anita has an interest and an aptitude *for* her work.

BUT: Anita has an interest *in* and an aptitude *for* her work. (Commas may be used in this construction: He has an interest in, and an aptitude for, his work.)

NOT: The teacher was puzzled and concerned *about* the student's behavior.

BUT: The teacher was puzzled *by* and concerned *about* the student's behavior.

Many people think that split constructions are awkward; they recommend such revisions as these—

Anita has an interest in her work and an aptitude for it.

The teacher was puzzled by the student's behavior and concerned about it.

Prepositional Phrase

The prepositional phrase is the preposition plus its object plus any modifiers of the object. The object of the preposition may be a word, a phrase, or a clause; and the modifiers of the object may likewise be words, phrases, or clauses. The prepositional phrase functions most often as an adjective or an adverb; occasionally it may also serve as a noun.

Too many prepositional phrases make a sentence unwieldy and hard to understand. In addition, they give the writer a real problem—the problem of putting each phrase as close as possible to the word it modifies. If you use verbs in the active voice you will find this problem greatly simplified. Compare these two sentences:

PASSIVE VOICE: This matter should be looked into *by your office* and a report furnished to us *on the case at the earliest possible date.*

ACTIVE VOICE: Please look *into this matter* and let us have a report *as soon as possible.*

Conjunctions, Relative Pronouns, and Relative Adverbs

These three types of connectives perform two distinctly different functions: some of them connect coordinate sentence elements (elements of equal grammatical rank); others both introduce a subordinate element and connect it with the rest of the sentence.

Three types of conjunctions connect coordinate elements:

COORDINATE CONJUNCTIONS

and	but	or
for	so	yet
nor		

CORRELATIVE CONJUNCTIONS

neither ... nor	either ... or
both ... and	if... then
since ... therefore	whether ... or
not only ... but also	

CONJUNCTIVE ADVERBS

therefore	otherwise	hence
nevertheless	however	besides
accordingly		

When connecting a subordinate element, the function of the subordinating clause governs the type of connective to be used in introducing it:

Adverb clauses are introduced by *subordinating conjunctions*—as, since, because, if, provided, after, before, where

Noun clauses are introduced by *relative pronouns*—that, whether, whichever, whatever, whoever

Adjective clauses are introduced by either *relative adverbs* (where, when, while) or *relative pronouns* (who, whom, which, that)

The rest of the chapter will help you to—

determine whether constructions are or are not *grammatically* coordinate

identify constructions that are subordinate

recognize connectives that can be used to tell the reader whether the constructions are considered to be coordinate or subordinate

avoid the misuse of connectives.

Connecting Elements of Equal Rank (Coordinate Elements)

Use Parallelism to Show Coordination

Sentence elements are said to be *coordinate* (or *parallel*) when they are of equal rank (of equal importance) both grammatically and logically. Determining equal *grammatical* importance is relatively simple:

words = words
phrases = phrases
subordinate clauses = subordinate clauses
principal clauses = principal clauses

Determining equal *logical* importance is more difficult. This requires that you weigh the importance of the thoughts you are expressing. Only you can determine this value, and you signal your reader by choosing the type of connective that makes your decision clear.

Elements not grammatically equal (not parallel):

His main virtues are *that he is sincere* and his *generosity*. (a clause linked to a word)

Improved:

> His main virtues are *that he is sincere* and *that he is generous.* (two noun clauses; noun clause = noun clause)

> His main virtues are his *sincerity* and his *generosity.* (two words)

Elements not equal in importance:

> Please advise us if our assumption is incorrect, and a further credit to your account will be made.

Improved:

> If our assumption is incorrect, please advise us and we will make a further credit to your account.

Use Coordinate Conjunctions to Show Coordination (Parallelism)

The coordinate conjunctions—and, but, or, nor, for, so, yet—are the connectives most frequently used to show that two ideas are equal (are parallel). Notice in the following illustrations that the two ideas connected are parallel.

> The President *and* the Vice President will attend. (connecting a word with a word)

> The candidate is a person of great capability *but* of little experience. (connecting a phrase with a phrase)

> The personnel director said that she had sent the candidate a letter *but* that she had not heard anything further in reply. (connecting a subordinate clause with a subordinate clause)

> I was eager to attend the seminar, *for* I knew that the exchange of ideas would be helpful. (connecting an independent clause with an independent clause)

Use Correlative Conjunctions to Show Coordination (Parallelism)

The correlative conjunctions—either...or, neither...nor, not only...but also, both...and, if...then, since...therefore—work in pairs to show that words and ideas are parallel (equal in importance).

> *Either* the mother *or* the father must attend the conference with the teacher. (connecting a word with a word)

> The report is designed *not only* to present a list of the problems facing us *but also* to recommend possible solutions to these problems. (connecting a phrase with a phrase)

The significant point which you should bear in mind when you use pairs of correlatives is that each member of the pair must be followed by the same part of speech (same grammatical construction). That is, if *not only is* followed by a verb, then *but also* must be followed by a verb; if *either* is followed by a phrase, *or* must likewise be followed by a phrase.

> NOT: *Either* cases of this type are much fewer in number *or* are not accompanied by the same medical problems. (*Either* is followed by a noun, *cases; or* is followed by a verb phrase.)
>
> BUT: Cases of this type *either* are much fewer in number *or* are not accompanied by the same medical problems.

> NOT: The reply *not only* was prompt *but also* complete.
>
> BUT: The reply was *not only* prompt *but also* complete.

When this plan is not followed, the result is "faulty parallelism." To turn faulty parallelism into effective parallelism, sometimes we need add only a word or two.

> NOT: The project was a disappointment *not only* to me *but also* my assistant. (*Not only* is followed by the prepositional phrase *to me; but also is* followed by a noun.)
>
> BUT: *The project was* a disappointment *not only* to me *but also* to my assistant. (Note that each of the correlative conjunctions is followed by a prepositional phrase.)

> NOT: The job was *both* to conduct the course *and* the evaluation of it.
>
> BUT: The job was *both* to conduct the course *and* to evaluate it.

Use Conjunctive Adverbs to Show Coordination

The conjunctive adverbs—therefore, however, consequently, accordingly, furthermore, besides, moreover, nevertheless, still— serve the double purpose of connecting independent clauses and of showing relationship between the clauses. Although the clause introduced by a conjunctive adverb is *grammatically independent,* it is *logically dependent* on the preceding clause for its complete meaning.

The conjunctive adverb has more modifying force than the coordinate conjunction but less connecting force. Therefore, the clauses joined by a conjunctive adverb are not so closely related as are those joined by a coordinate conjunction. Clauses joined by a conjunctive adverb must be separated by a semicolon or a period.

> The curriculum has not yet been published; *nevertheless,* we must proceed with the preparation of the course.

> The meeting was held at 3 o'clock; *however,* I was not able to attend.

Certain phrases—such as *on the contrary, on the other hand, in the first place, in fact, in addition, for this reason, for example, at the same time, in the interim*—have the same modifying and connective force as conjunctive adverbs.

> The new proposal may be a solution to our financial problem; on the other hand, it may only make the problem worse.

> We discussed the items on the agenda. In addition, several members proposed new topics.

Use Punctuation to Show Coordination

The semicolon may be substituted for the connective between coordinate elements.

> I have almost finished these e-mails; there are only three more to reply to.

> The reception of this course will be interesting to watch; it is the first of its kind to he offered.

Connecting Elements of Unequal Rank (Connecting Subordinate Elements with Principal Elements)

In the previous section we discussed how to put ideas of equal importance into structures that show they are equal. But many of our sentences contain ideas not equal in importance which should be expressed in a way that emphasizes their relationship. Weigh the ideas in your sentence to determine which are basic to the purpose of the sentence and to the goal of the whole writing and which are less important. Then make this distinction clear by putting the less important ideas into subordinate constructions.

Use Subordinating Conjunctions to Show Subordination

Subordinating conjunctions—as, because, since, as though, than, although, provided, if, unless, how, after, before, so that, in order that, when, while, until—introduce adverb clauses and connect them to independent clauses. The subordinating conjunction shows a relationship between the clauses it connects.

I must miss that meeting, *even though* I would like to attend.

If the project is to be finished on time, we must have those figures by Friday.

The official will call the play *after* the replay is reviewed.

Use Relative Pronouns to Show Subordination

Some relative pronouns—*who, whom, which, that*—introduce adjective clauses. Others—primarily *that* and the compound relative pronouns *whichever, whatever, whoever, whomever*—introduce noun clauses. Both types of relative pronouns connect the clause they introduce to the rest of the sentence.

The applicant *who* called for an appointment has arrived.

A program *that* is operating properly is a great help to the computer user.

The officer to *whom* I wrote has since left the company. Give the package to *whoever* answers the door.

The manager will tell us *whatever* we need to know about the new system.

Use Relative Adverbs to Show Subordination

The relative adverbs—*where, when, while*—introduce adjective clauses and connect them to the rest of the sentence.

This is the building *where* the office is located.

This is the time of year *when* we are particularly busy.

List of Troublesome Connectives

And vs. Also

Also, a weak connective, should not be used in place of *and* in sentences such as:

NOT: The vice-president writes letters, memorandums, also some procedures.

BUT: The vice-president writes letters, memorandums, and some procedures.

And Etc.

The abbreviation *etc.* stands for the Latin *et cetera,* meaning *and so forth.* Obviously, then, an additional *and* is not only unnecessary but incorrect.

NOT: The office manager requisitioned paper, pens, print cartridges *and etc.*

BUT: He requisitioned paper, pens, print cartridges, *etc.*

And Which, And Who, But Which

Avoid using *and which, and who, but which, but that,* etc. when there is no preceding *who, which,* or *that* in the sentence to complete the parallel construction.

NOT: We are looking for a program more economical to operate *and which* will be easy to use.

BUT: We are looking for a program *which* will be more economical to operate *and which* will be easy to use.

OR: We are looking for a program more economical to operate and easy to use.

Too Many And's

Avoid stringing together a group of sentence elements connected by *ands.*

NOT: The evaluation of the training program was planned and conducted and reported to the coaching staff.

BUT: The evaluation of the training program was planned and conducted; then it was reported to the coaching staff.

OR: The evaluation of the training program was planned, conducted, and reported to the coaching staff.

And vs. But

Use *and* to show addition; use *but* to show contrast.

NOT: The buyer and the assistant have been called to a meeting, *and* the supervisor will be in the office all afternoon.

BUT: The buyer and the assistant have been called to a meeting, *but* the supervisor will be in the office all afternoon.

Avoid using *but* to show contrast when the negative idea is already present in the sentence through the use of some other word.

NOT: In vain we tried to convince him, *but* we were unable to do it. (The phrase *in vain* already expresses the negative idea.)

BUT: *In vain* we tried to convince him.

OR: We tried to convince him, *but* we were unable to.

Coordinate Conjunctions or Conjunctive Adverbs to Begin a Sentence

A sentence or a paragraph may begin with *and, but,* or any other coordinating conjunction. A coordinate conjunction or a conjunctive adverb at the beginning of a sentence is often a handy signpost for the reader, telling him in which direction this new sentence will carry him.

However, when beginning a sentence with a coordinating conjunction or conjunctive adverb, check to see that you have written a complete sentence with a subject and a verb. If you have not done so, your sentence is a fragment error.

As, Since, Because

These conjunctions can be used interchangeably to introduce clauses of cause or reason.

Because the book was due at the library, I returned it.

Since the book was due at the library, I returned it.

As the book was due at the library, I returned it.

However, *since* and *as* have another function—*since* introduces clauses of sequence of time, and *as* introduces clauses of duration of time. Because of the double function of these two words, we must be careful to use them only in sentences in which they cannot be misunderstood.

NOT: *Since* this report was prepared to analyze the effects of...(could mean: Since the time that this report was prepared...)

BUT: *Because* this report was prepared to analyze the effects of...

NOT: As I was typing the monthly grades, he gave the assignment to Beth. (could mean: During the time that I was typing the monthly-grades ...)

BUT: *Because* I was typing the monthly grades...

When an *as* or *since* clause comes last in the sentence, the meaning of the conjunction can be made clear by the punctuation of the clause. If *as* or *since* is used as a time indicator, the clause it intro-duces is not set off from the sentence. But if the conjunction intro-duces a clause of cause or reason, the clause is set off.

> There have been several changes in the menu since the com-mittee released its findings. (No punctuation; *since* means *since the time that*)

> There have been several changes in the menu, since the com-mittee released its findings. (...*because* the committee released its findings)

As vs. That or Whether

Avoid using *as* in place of *that* or *whether* to introduce clauses following such verbs as *say, think, know.*

> NOT: I don't know *as* I believe you.
> BUT: I don't know *whether* I believe you.

If vs. Whether

If is used to introduce clauses of condition or supposition.

> We will go *if* the babysitter arrives on time.
> *If* you cannot answer the letter immediately, please call me.

Whether introduces clauses indicating an alternative. The alter-native may be expressed in the sentence or understood.

> It will not make any difference *whether* they agree or disagrees with the proposal.

> Please let me know *whether* you received the check.

Sometimes you can use either *if* or *whether* in such constructions as:

> Please let me know *if* (or *whether*) you received the check.

> I wonder *if* (or *whether*) they will attend.

> I don't know *if* (or *whether*) they deserve an award.

Most people, however, prefer *whether* when there is any danger that the reader may fail to understand the meaning.

Whether vs. Whether or Not

It is not essential that *or not* be used with *whether* to complete the alternative choice. Often, to do so is unnecessarily wordy. These words may be added if they are needed for emphasis.

EITHER: Please let me know *whether or not* you received our letter.

OR: Please me know *whether* you received our letter.

Omission of That

That may be omitted in noun clauses (especially those following such verbs as *say, think, feel, believe, hope*) and in adjective clauses if the meaning of the sentence is clear.

NOUN CLAUSES:
The promoter said (that) the singer would call me before noon.
I hope (that) we can finish this project today.

ADJECTIVE CLAUSES:
The book (that) I asked for is out on loan.
The instructions (that) they gave were perfectly clear.

Faulty Repetition of That

Do not use *that* twice to introduce the same noun clause. This error most often occurs in a long sentence in which a long interrupting expression occurs between the *that* and the rest of its clause.

NOT: I am sure you can appreciate *that*, in order to protect the interests of all alumni as well as the interests of the administration, *that* we must establish whether the original policies were correctly applied.

BUT: I am sure you can appreciate *that*, in order to protect the interests of all alumni as well as the interests of the administration, we must establish whether the original policies were correctly applied.

When

Avoid using *when* to introduce a definition unless the definition pertains to time.

NOT: Their first important step in the improvement of the highway was *when* they thoroughly surveyed the situation. (The step was not *when*.)

BUT: Their first important step in the improvement of the highway was *the thorough survey* of the situation.

CORRECT: Three o'clock is *when* the meeting will be held.

Where

Avoid using *where* to introduce a definition unless the definition pertains to place or location.

NOT: A sentence is *where* you have a subject and a verb. (A sentence is not *where*.)

BUT: A sentence is a group of words containing a subject and a verb.

CORRECT: The large conference room is *where* the meeting is being held.

Note: Avoid Substituting *Where* for *That*.

NOT: I saw in the paper *where* the new player has been put into the lineup.

BUT: I saw in the paper *that* the new player has been put into the lineup.

While vs. When

While indicates duration of time; *when* indicates a fixed or stated period of time.

When I return to the office, I will call the dean. (at that fixed time)

While I am at the office, I will look for that information. (During the time that I am at the office...)

While vs. Though, Although, and But

While pertains to time and should not be substituted loosely for though, although, whereas, and but.

> NOT: *While* I did not remember his friend's name, I thought I could recognize her face.
>
> BUT: *Although* I did not remember his friend's name, I thought I could recognize her face.

> NOT: I assembled the material for the presentation *while* he wrote the outline. (Could mean: during the time that he...)
>
> BUT: I assembled the material for the presentation, *but* he wrote the outline.

Quiz

Connectives are vital to convey meaning. Review your knowledge of proper use of connectives with this quiz.

Directions: Read the following sentences, looking for problems with connectives. If you find an error, rewrite the sentence. If the sentence is correct, write "correct."

1. This year's Super Bowl will be played at the stadium at San Diego.

2. Our seats are three rows underneath the last row of the orchestra section.

3. That situation is one which I will not put up with.

4. Karen is eligible and interested in the new program.

5. The person chosen must be competent and trustworthy.

6. I am very trustworthy but of little experience in this area.

7. Either use e-mail or send a fax to return the information to me.

8. With your order, you will receive a free strainer also a grater.

9. An eponym is when a person's name becomes the source of a word.

10. An epigraph is an inscription on a statue, or it is a quotation at the beginning of a work of literature.

Answers and Explanations

1. This year's Super Bowl will be played *in* the stadium in San Diego. *In* is used to refer to the interior of a structure and before geographical place names.

2. Our seats are three rows *below* the last row of the orchestra section. Idiom explains the change, but so does logic. *Below* suggests three rows forward. *Underneath* would mean they were under the floor.

3. Correct. The situation is one I will not put *up with*. There is no rule forbidding a sentence's ending with a preposition.

4. Karen is eligible *for* and interested in the new program. In a split construction in which two words are completed by different prepositions, use both prepositions.

5. Correct. The person chosen must be *competent and trustworthy*. The two words are grammatically parallel and of equal importance in meaning.

6. I am very trustworthy, but I *have* little experience in this area. The original sentence violates parallel construction because the objects of the verb are an adjective, trustworthy, and a prepositional phrase, *of little experience*.

7. Correct. Either *use e-mail* or *send a fax* to return the information to me. Use parallel construction with correlative conjunctions.

8. With your order, you will receive a free strainer *and* a grater. Do not use *also* when you mean *and*.

9. An eponym *is a word* whose source is a person's name. Do not use *is when* or *is where* in definitions.

10. Correct. An epigraph is an inscription on a statue, or it is a quotation at the beginning of a work of literature. The definition does not use *is when* or *is where*. The elements joined by the coordinating conjunction *or* are parallel.

8

PUNCTUATION AND GOOD SENTENCES

Punctuation probably gives us more trouble than any other area of writing—yet, correctly used, it can also give us more help in clearly expressing our ideas. We have no more useful tool than punctuation for showing the relationship of the parts of our sentences and, thus, of our thoughts.

The Importance of Punctuation

Punctuation is an important part of writing. However, there is a trend toward using less punctuation. This trend doesn't prove that punctuation is becoming less important: instead, it shows that sentences are becoming shorter and simpler, that there are not so many twists and turns in our sentences—turns that need to be marked for the bewildered reader. If you want to use less punctuation, go ahead. Just be sure yours are not the long, involved sentences that need lots of punctuation to keep the reader on the right road. Remember, the sentences that need little punctuation are the straightforward, simple ones.

Since punctuation is a part of writing, the only one who can effectively punctuate a piece of writing is the person who writes it. Only the writers know the relationships they want their punctuation to express.

This chapter approaches the understanding of punctuation by two routes: first, by discussing what to punctuate; and second, by listing the punctuation marks. The first part discusses what sentence elements we need to punctuate and how we may effectively punctuate them. The balance of the chapter lists the punctuation marks and their uses.

Punctuation

Functional punctuation is essential to clear writing. Most of the punctuation in our sentences can be grouped by function into:

(1) Punctuation that *separates* one idea from another so that the reader may see them directly:
The report was accurate, but it was not well organized.

(2) Punctuation that *encloses* incidental or parenthetic expressions:
My letter of July 6, *a copy of which is attached,* should answer your question.

(3) Punctuation that *emphasizes* certain sentence elements by setting them apart from the rest of the sentence. (These elements are often out of natural order for increased emphasis.)
This book, *newly revised,* is now available. (In natural order—this newly revised book—the element is emphasized less.)

The comma is the mark that most often performs these functions. And the comma, because of its wide use, is the mark most often misused. We may be able to avoid some errors in punctuation by applying this formula for the use of the comma (it is valid, too, for other marks): *Use one comma to separate; use two commas to enclose.*

Separating Main Clauses

Main clauses (also called principal or independent clauses) are those that may stand alone as sentences. When combined with other main clauses, they form compound sentences. Within certain limitations, the choice of what punctuation to use to separate main clauses is up to you. You know best how closely related—or how widely separated—are the ideas expressed by the clauses you have written. And it is up to you to choose the punctuation that will come closest to conveying your meaning to the reader.

How do you decide what punctuation to use? By weighing these factors: Is there a conjunction between the clauses? If so, what kind of conjunction is it? How closely related are the clauses? How important is the thought expressed by each clause? How much emphasis do we wish to give to each clause?

The punctuation marks that may be used to separate clauses are: the period, the colon, the dash, the semicolon, and the comma. The comma may be used, however, *only* when the clauses have been linked by a connective. (A violation of this use of the comma is called the *comma splice* or the *run-on sentence*.)

Showing Close Relationship between Clauses

To show the closest possible relationship between clauses and to give the least amount of emphasis to the individual clauses, use the coordinate conjunctions *and, or,* or *for* with the comma.

> The passenger's baggage has been lost, and the claim on it was filed yesterday.

If the clauses are short enough and the relationship is clear enough, we do not need any punctuation mark.

> The passenger's baggage is lost and the claim has been filed.

Even when the relationship is close, we usually use a comma before the coordinate conjunction *for* to avoid confusing it with the preposition *for*.

> The passenger has not yet filed his claim, for the search has not been completed.

And before the coordinate conjunctions *but, yet,* and *nor* to heighten the idea of contrast expressed by these conjunctions.

> The passenger's baggage was lost last week, but the claim on it has not yet been filed.

Emphasizing Individual Clauses by Using a Period

To give the most emphasis to the individual clauses—when the thought relationship of the clauses is not especially close—separate them by a period, making each a simple sentence.

> The meeting was over. The committee members had returned to their hotels. Some had even left town.

Clauses may be separated by a period, even when the clauses need a conjunction to express the exact relationship between them. Using a period between the clauses, even when a conjunction is present, emphasizes the individual clauses by calling the reader's full attention to each one.

The paper was submitted to the teacher last week, with the expectation that it would be marked immediately. But no grades have been posted yet.

When the conjunction is a conjunctive adverb, it does not have to appear first in the clause.

The paper was submitted to the teacher last week with the expectation that it would be marked immediately. As yet, *however*, no grades have been given.

Emphasizing Individual Clauses by Using a Semicolon

If the relationship between two clauses is clear without a conjunction—and if the relationship is a close one—we may separate the clauses by a semicolon.

The union evidently arrived at several solutions to this problem; their report was submitted to management yesterday.

The semicolon is also used to separate clauses linked by a conjunctive adverb, whether the adverb appears between or in the body of the second clause.

The paper was submitted to the teacher last week with the expectation that it would be marked immediately; however, no grades have been posted yet.

Expressing Special Relationships

Introductory main clauses

You may use either the colon or the dash between an introductory clause and a second clause which completes or explains what the first clause says.

It is just as Carl predicted—as hard as we worked, we were not able to complete the building on time.

We can present the information in either of two ways: we can deliver the report in person, or we can prepare a written report.

The Semicolon with the Coordinate Conjunction

You may use a semicolon between two clauses linked by a coordinate conjunction:

(1) when the clauses contain commas:

We will, of course, attempt to finish the construction by the deadline; but, as you know, we have had several serious delays.

(2) when we wish to emphasize one clause in a sentence that contains three main clauses:

The money has been allotted, and the office has been decorated; and now the real work begins.

The Comma with No Conjunction

We may use a comma:

(1) to separate the two parts of an echo question:
You didn't believe me, did you?
That was your attorney, wasn't it?

(2) to separate short parallel clauses:
The thunder roared, the lightning flashed, the rains came.
Some people liked it, more didn't.
It's a bird, it's a plane, it's Superman.

SUMMARY

Here, in diagram form, and in the order in which they are discussed above, are the ways in which we may separate main clauses using the period, the colon, the dash, the semicolon, and the comma.

To show close relationship between clauses:
********* and *********.

********** , and *********.
********** , for *********.
********** , but *********.
********** , nor *********.

To emphasize individual clauses—use a period to separate:
********** *********.
**********. But *********.
**********. However, *********.
**********. ***, however, ***.

To emphasize individual clauses—use a semicolon to separate:
**********; *********.
**********; however, *********.
**********; ***, however, ******.

To express special relationships:
Introductory Main Clauses
**********—*********.
**********. *********.

The Semicolon with the Coordinate Conjunction
, ***, ***, and ***, **.
**********, and *********; and *********.

The Comma with No Conjunction
**********, *****? (echo question)
********** *********, *********.

Enclosing Modifiers and Appositives

There are three sets of punctuation marks to enclose a modifier, an appositive, or any other expression that interrupts the flow of the sentence.

The *comma* is the mark most frequently used for this purpose. It is the lightest of the three possible marks, indicating only a slight separation in thought between the element enclosed and the rest of the sentence.

That textbook, *which was published less than a year ago*, is already out of print.

The *dash* emphasizes the element being enclosed. It may also be used, even when no special emphasis is needed, to enclose an element containing internal commas.

> Ms. Holtzman—*who has never taken a day of sick leave in 32 years*—is at home today with a cold. (Element enclosed by dashes for emphasis)

> Ms. Holtzman—*you remember, the woman who welcomed you when you first came to work here*—is retiring next week. (Element contains internal punctuation)

Parentheses indicate that the element being enclosed is only loosely connected with the thought of the sentence. Parentheses usually enclose material meant for reference or explanation.

> In spite of the governor's resistance (*which still continues strong*), the plan was adopted.

> M. Katz's latest book (*published by Arco*) will be available later this month.

Below are three variations of the same sentence. Notice the degrees of emphasis you may give the enclosed element by your choice of punctuation.

> The gray stone building, *built in 1980,* which has housed our offices for the past two years is scheduled to be torn down next year.

> The gray stone building—*built in 1980*—which has housed our offices for the past two years is scheduled to be torn down next year.

> The gray stone building (*built in 1980*) which has housed our offices for the past two years is scheduled to be torn down next year.

Restrictive and Nonrestrictive Modifiers

Modifiers and appositives are classed as *restrictive* or as *nonrestrictive*. A *restrictive modifier* or *appositive* cannot be omitted without changing the meaning of the sentence. It restricts or limits the word preceding it, and by answering the question *Which one?* it also serves an identifying function. Because restrictive modifiers are essential parts of the sentence, they are not set off by commas.

A *nonrestrictive modifier* or *appositive*, on the other hand, is not essential to the meaning of the sentence. It may add interesting or helpful information, but it is not necessary as a restrictive modifier is. To show that they contain ideas of secondary importance, nonrestrictive modifiers are set off by commas.

Adjective Modifiers

Restrictive adjective clauses, verbal phrases, and prepositional phrases are not set off from the rest of the sentence by commas. Nonrestrictive modifiers are.

RESTR: The employee *who wrote that letter* is on leave today.

NONR: Mr. Velasquez, *who wrote that letter*, is on leave today.

RESTR: The new sales representative *from Milwaukee* is doing a good job.

NONR: Mr. Velasquez, *from Milwaukee*, is new to this office.

RESTR: An office in a building *built in 1960* may not meet the needs of today's executive.

NONR: That red brick structure, *built in 1960*, is scheduled for demolition.

Logic will sometimes tell the reader whether a modifier is restrictive or nonrestrictive, the punctuation serving only to point up what is already obvious. But sometimes a sentence may have two possible meanings, depending upon whether the modifier is considered restrictive or nonrestrictive. In these cases the reader is entirely dependent on your correct punctuation of the modifier.

RESTR: His estate was willed to his daughters *who had not married* and to his son. (This sentence says that only his *unmarried* daughters were included in the will; any *married* daughters received no part of the estate.)

NONR: His estate was willed to his daughters, *who had not married*, and to his son. (This sentence says that all his daughters—who, incidentally, were not married—were included in the will.)

Adverbial Modifiers

Adverbial modifiers are not always clearly restrictive or nonrestrictive. Often only you can determine whether an adverbial modifier is essential to the meaning of the sentence. Then, too, the punctuation of adverbial modifiers is not solely dependent upon whether the modifier is restrictive or nonrestrictive. Factors such as the position and length of the modifier and the amount of emphasis it should have also play a part.

As a general rule you should not set off a restrictive adverbial modifier that occurs at the end of the sentence.

I have not heard from Jan *since last Thursday.*

Jan will not miss the meeting *if we send a reminder note.*

What is the procedure *under these circumstances?*

Updike was in his early fifties *when he won a Pulitzer Prize.*

Both restrictive and nonrestrictive adverbial modifiers are usually set off if they come at the beginning of the sentence.

If we send Jan a reminder note, he will not miss the meeting.

When he won a Pulitzer prize, Updike was in his early fifties.

You may or may not set off a nonrestrictive adverbial modifier that comes at the end of the sentence. Ordinarily you should set it off if it is long or if it needs special emphasis.

This project must be finished on time, *even if it means overtime for the whole staff.*

The bill is expected to pass, *although there is strong opposition to it in some quarters.*

This is all the information we have, *so far as I know.*

We have three ways of punctuating an adverbial clause or phrase which immediately follows a conjunction:

(1) no punctuation:
The senator is planning to attend, but *if the time is changed* she will have to cancel.

(2) punctuation after the modifier only:
I may have a slight cash surplus; and *if no more urgent use for the money arises before the end of the month*, I may buy a DVD player.

(3) punctuation before and after the modifier:
We are working hard now; but, *if the building is approved*, we will have twice as much work to do.

Appositives

Restrictive appositives—those necessary for identification—are not separated from the word they stand in apposition to. Nonrestrictive appositives are set off.

RESTR: My brother *James* will arrive Friday. (James is one of several brothers.)

NONR: My brother, *James*, will arrive Friday. (My only brother, whose name is James.)

RESTR: Hemingway's novel *For Whom the Bell Tolls* was presented on television. (Setting off the title by commas would indicate that this is Hemingway's only novel.)

NONR: One of Hemingway's novels, *For Whom the Bell Tolls*, was presented on television.

Often an introductory expression—such as *namely, for instance, that is to say, in other words, for example, such as*—is used to emphasize an appositive. Below are some of the ways we may punctuate these expressions:

> One of the officers, *namely Henderson*, was on duty.

> A nonrestrictive, *or nonessential*, appositive is set off.

> This has presented us with a new problem: *specifically, the lack of time.*

> Our office is instituting several new techniques—*the revised filing procedures, for example.*

> The extremes in architecture (*that is, the very modern and the very old fashioned*) do not appeal to me.

Punctuating Introductory Elements

Adverbial Clauses and Verbal Phrases

An introductory adverbial clause or verbal phrase is usually set off from the rest of the sentence, even when it is restrictive.

> *When you go to the supply room*, bring me some copy paper.

> *If you call me before noon*, I can meet you for lunch.

> *Generally speaking*, we approve these requests.

> *To reach my office*, take the elevator to the third floor.

If the clause or phrase is quite short and if there is no danger that it might be misread, the comma may be omitted.

Prepositional Phrases

Introductory prepositional phrases should be followed by a comma unless they are short and omitting the comma will not cause confusion.

> *Near the busy airport*, long term parking facilities provided convenience for travelers.

> *In Los Angeles* many such facilities are on Century Boulevard.

Introductory Elements with Connective Force

If the element is obviously parenthetical, separate it from the rest of the sentence.

In the light of this report, we must review our entire lineup.

On the other hand, this may have been a hasty decision.

As a result, we will have to postpone our planned meeting.

On the contrary, they may have an answer for us by Thursday.

However, we must not plan on anything as risky as that.

But if the expression is short and closely connected with the thought of the sentence, separating it will only destroy the smoothness of the sentence.

Last month my productivity was higher than it has been all year.

Possibly we may be able to beat last year's record.

Thus we will establish a new high in production.

Punctuating Parenthetical Elements

By *parenthetical* we mean any element that interrupts the flow of the sentence. Some of the elements we discussed in earlier sections may be considered parenthetical. This section will list some others—elements that are not needed for grammatical completeness but that are related to the thought of the sentence. Parenthetical elements are set off from the rest of the sentence—in most instances by commas. If the parenthetical element occurs in the middle of the sentence, be sure that it is preceded and followed by a punctuation mark.

Interrupting Transitional Expressions

We were able, *fortunately*, to complete the decorating before the party.

The room, *therefore*, looked festive.

This, *however*, was impossible.

We will, *of course*, be happy to help you.

This, *on the other hand*, should be easier.

I was, *as a matter of fact*, planning to call you.

Interrupting Expressions Identifying Speaker or Source

This game, *we feel*, is our most important one.

The team, *it is now believed*, will win the title.

The series, *as you know*, will begin next Monday.

This report, *I might say*, is the best you have done.

"The party," *the host said*, "was an outstanding success."

Addresses, Dates, Titles

Please send applications to the Personnel Division, *Room 1500, Senate Office Building, Washington, D. C.*

Lee is a member of the Alexandria, *Virginia*, Chamber of Commerce.

I read it in a Baltimore, *Maryland*, newspaper.

The representatives will be from Chicago, *Illinois*; Omaha, *Nebraska*; Salem, *Oregon*; Austin, *Texas*.

Your letter of July 6, *2002*, arrived while I was on vacation. (If the day is not included, the month and year are usually written with no punctuation: *July 2002*).

Ms. Andrea M. Green, *chair of the club*, will speak at the opening ceremonies.

Nominative Absolute

All things being equal, I believe she will win.

There being no further discussion, the meeting was adjourned.

The measure having been passed by a large majority, the chairman went on to the next item.

Words in Direct Address

Tell me, *Doctor*, how serious is it?

With your permission, *Mr. President*, I would like to ask another question.

Separating Coordinate Items in Series

Separate coordinate items in series by punctuation unless they are joined by coordinate conjunctions. The comma is the mark most often used, although we may use the semicolon to separate items containing internal commas and the dash to throw strong emphasis on the individual items.

Series with Coordinate Conjunction

When the items are connected by coordinate conjunctions, they do not usually need any punctuation. But we may punctuate if the series is long or if we want to emphasize the items.

EITHER: The instructor and the students and the rest of the faculty heard the discussion.

OR: The instructor, and the students, and all the faculty that were able to attend heard the discussion.

Series with No Connective

To make the meaning clear, we need to separate the items in a series containing no connectives.

My ambition now is to get away from the office, to lie on the beach, to listen to the surf.

Series with Connective Joining Last Two Members

A series with a connective joining the last two members may be punctuated in either of two ways:

EITHER: The trainer ordered instructional videos, audio tapes, and manuals.

OR: The trainer ordered instructional videos, audio tapes and manuals.

EITHER: Every piece of writing has a beginning, a middle, and an end.

OR: Every piece of writing has a beginning, a middle and an end.

Most editors prefer the use of the comma before the connective because this punctuation leaves no doubt in the reader's mind that the last two members of the series are to be considered separately.

Consecutive Adjectives (Two or More)

Separate by commas only those consecutive adjectives which are coordinate. Adjectives are coordinate if (1) they can be linked by *and* and (2) they independently modify the substantive.

Coordinate (each adjective independently modifies the substantive):

a lengthy, overdue report (a lengthy *and* overdue report; an overdue *and* lengthy report)

a careful, painstaking review

a busy, ambitious, clever technician

Not coordinate (each adjective modifies all that follows it):

the new statistical chart (not: new *and* statistical)

three small fresh lemons (small modifies fresh, and three modifies small fresh lemons)

a green ballpoint pen

The Punctuation Marks

This section is for reference and review and lists the punctuation marks with their major functions.

Use the Period

... to mark the end of a sentence that is not a question or an exclamation.

The plane arrived earlier than expected.

... after a request—to distinguish it from a direct question.

Will you please send us three copies of the January 17 issue.

Will you let us know whether you can join us for lunch.

... after words or phrases that stand as sentences. (This is not an endorsement of fragmentary sentences, but if sentence fragments must be used, they are followed by periods.)

True.

What time will you be back? By noon.

... after abbreviations and initials.

R.J. Pale, M.D., is employed by the Central Medical Association.

... to show that material has been omitted from a quotation. Omissions are usually shown by three periods, in addition to any other punctuation needed at that point in the material. Three periods are called an ellipsis.

Her reply was, "Don't worry ... since I feel better."

His reply was, "Don't worry about me anymore..."

Use the Question Mark

... after a sentence that asks a *direct question*. (Not after a request, even though it is phrased as a question.)

Have you heard from Ms. Rollins this morning?

You know the letter I mean, don't you?

But: He asked where Ms. Rollins was. (indirect question)

... to indicate doubt about the correctness of a statement.

The company was established in 1990(?) and was incorporated in 1991.

About a year after the company was established (1990?), it was incorporated.

Use the Exclamation Point

... after an exclamatory sentence or remark, to show strong feeling. (The exclamation point should be used sparingly—rarely in expository writing.)

That's the longest bridge I've seen yet!

Whew! What a day!

Use the Comma

... to separate main clauses joined by a coordinate conjunction.

The movie has ended, and the crowd has left.

The movie is over, but the crowd is still inside.

The movie is over, yet the crowd remains.

... to separate short, parallel main clauses not joined by a coordinate conjunction.

The table was cleared, the coffee was brought out, the dessert service began.

... to separate the two independent clauses of an echo question.

You thought I'd be late, didn't you?

... to set off a nonrestrictive adjective modifier.

The technician, *whom you met last week*, will help you.

The Grey Company, *established in 1899*, is the city's oldest business firm.

Exhausted from a long day of meetings, she stuffed some papers into her portfolio and left for the airport.

Elated, she called her husband in to tell him the news.

... to set off a nonrestrictive adverbial modifier at the end of a sentence, especially if it is long or needs special emphasis.

I will call you at 4 o'clock, *after the messenger brings the mail*.

I have not seen him since Tuesday, *when he spoke at the luncheon*.

I must finish this book report by tomorrow, *even if I have to work on it all night*.

... to set off a nonrestrictive appositive.

My brother, *Scott*, has been visiting me.

Alisha, *my younger sister*, has been visiting me.

Office equipment, *such as copying machines and calculators*, should be shut down when not in use.

... to set off an introductory adverbial modifier.

When you get home, look up that information and call me.

If your balance is correct, we will have enough money left to buy that new DVD player.

Because she was familiar with the new computer, she was able to compile the data on time.

... to set off an introductory prepositional phrase.

In spite of his cold, he put in a full day at the office.

In the light of her objections, we may reconsider the proposed trade.

… to set off an introductory transitional expression that is not closely related to the meaning of the sentence.

On the other hand, this article may be based on nothing more than opinion.

In the first place, we do not have the money to take a vacation right now.

… to set off an interrupting transitional expression.

We may, *of course*, postpone the game indefinitely.

We must be sure, *however*, that the public understands our reasons.

… to set off an interrupting expression identifying speaker or source.

A little change of pace, *we decided*, was just what we needed.

That, *I feel*, may be the root of our problem.

"Your organization," *Chris said*, "has done an outstanding job."

… to set off addresses, dates, titles.

She moved to Omaha, *Nebraska*, shortly after she graduated.

Your letter of July 6, *1999*, explains the problem clearly.

… to set off a nominative absolute phrase.

The meal having been paid for, he felt he must eat it.

… to set off words in direct address.

Your letters are ready for signature, *Ms. Brown.*

May I interrupt, *Professor Lee*, to ask that the question be repeated.

… to separate coordinate items

He asked that a table, extra chairs, and coffee cups be placed in the office.

She said it had been an exciting, exhausting day.

Use the Semicolon

... to separate main clauses not joined by a coordinate conjunction.

We submitted the project plans to the contractor this morning; they were approved by noon.

The boss publicly commended us for our work; she is particularly pleased about the new marketing plan.

We have completed the first draft of the article; now we can revise it.

... to separate main clauses joined by a conjunctive adverb.

The revision is complete; however, the editor has not seen it yet.

... to separate main clauses joined by a coordinate conjunction when the clauses contain commas (if the semicolon is needed for clarity).

You will, of course, want to notify him; and, unless he is out of town, he will surely attend. (Comma after *and* is optional.)

She has placed her tentative order; but, naturally, she will wait until after the trial run to make a final decision.

... to emphasize one of the three main clauses in a sentence.

The plans have been made, and the restaurant has been chosen; now we are ready for the office party.

... to separate coordinate items in a series when the items contain internal commas.

Attending were representatives from Omaha, Nebraska; Los Angeles, California; Salem, Oregon; and San Francisco, California.

Meeting to discuss the new plan were: Wilson, just in from New York; Jackson, here only for the day; and Velez, only recently back from vacation.

Use the Colon

... between main clauses when the second clause completes or explains the first.

> There are two courses open to us: we can demand that the issue be reopened, or we can abide by the decision until the group meets again in the fall.

... after an expression that formally introduces a list, an explanation, or a quotation.

> Our new cook will need to possess three qualities: endurance, patience, and humor.

> Our supply list includes the following items: one ream of bond paper, one box of pencils, and three ink cartridges.

> In a talk the director said: "This film has, in the past few days, started to develop into a worthwhile project."

Use the Dash

... between main clauses when the second clause explains or summarizes the first.

> The decision was obvious—we would have to recall all samples until we could recheck them.

> He has done two things of which he is enormously proud—he has led the division to increased production, and he has helped increase the prestige of the division throughout the organization.

... to set off a nonrestrictive modifier or parenthetical element that contains internal commas.

> The Williams Building—built, it is believed, in 1900, was torn down three years ago.

... to emphasize a nonrestrictive modifier or parenthetical element that is normally set off by commas.

> She was—fortunately—able to deliver the pictures by the deadline.

I plan to ask Scott—who is the person who surely ought to know—why this party was organized.

... to set off a nonrestrictive appositive for special emphasis.

Only one person in the Senate—the vice-president—can break a tie vote.

There is just one thing wrong with my filing system—I can't find anything!

Use Parentheses

... to enclose a nonrestrictive modifier or parenthetic element that is only loosely connected with the thought of the sentence.

The book (published in 2002) has been most helpful to me.

The discussion of those principles (pages 44–49) is one of the best I've seen.

If other punctuation is needed at the place in the sentence where the parentheses occur, it follows the closing parenthesis. But if the punctuation pertains to the parenthetic matter it is placed within the parentheses.

If you plan to attend the convention (to be held at the Hilton Hotel), please notify us by June 1.

Use Quotation Marks

... to enclose any direct quotation, whether a single word, a sentence, or several paragraphs. Do not include within the quotation marks any explanatory expressions not a part of the quoted material.

The dentist described the new procedure as "long needed and much appreciated."

She thought the idea was "devastating."

... to enclose the entire quotation, not the individual sentences, when the quotation consists of several sentences.

"I am pleased with the progress we have been making in recent months. Our scoring is up, and morale seems to be high. All in all, we have come a long way since we first began this season," the coach said.

… before each paragraph of series of quoted paragraphs, but after only the final paragraph.

> " — — — — — — — — — — — — — — —
> — — — — — — — — — — — — — — — — .
> " — — — — — — — — — — — — — — —
> — — — — — — — — — — — — — — — — .
> " — — — — — — — — — — — — — — —
> — — — — — — — — — — — — — — — —
> — — — — — — — — ."

… to enclose the title of a published work that is part of a larger whole, such as an article from a magazine, a chapter from a book, a poem from a collection. The title of the complete work is usually italicized in printed copy and underlined in typed copy.

For examples of this style, read the chapter on "How to Hit Like a Pro" in Steve White's *Playing It Tough*.

Of interest to every executive is "How to Take the Tension Out of Your Daily Life," an article in the May issue of *Today's Health*.

Use single quotation marks to enclose a quotation within a quotation.

Arthur remarked, "The statement 'don't call too early' seems to leave a lot to the imagination."

When a quotation is given in indirect form, no quotation marks are used. An indirect quotation is usually introduced by *that*.

DIRECT QUOTATION: She said, "I mailed my manuscript yesterday."

INDIRECT QUOTATION: She said that she mailed her manuscript yesterday.

Quotation Mark with Other Marks of Punctuation

The comma and period are placed inside the quotation marks, whether or not they are a part of the quoted material.

"I wonder," he said, "if we will ever finish it."

There is one exception to the placing of the comma and period inside the quotation marks, regardless of whether they are a part of the quoted material. When you are writing about insertions in, or deletions from, certain legal work, such as laws and regulations, put the punctuation mark outside the quotation marks *unless it is a part of the material to be inserted or deleted.*

Insert the words "growth", "production", and "manufacture".

To be inserted immediately after the words "cadets, U.S. Coast Guard,".

The semicolon and colon are placed outside the quotation marks unless they are a part of the quoted matter.

"We have come far, but we have farther to go"; that is the note on which he began his speech.

I have only one thing to say about the Yeats' poem "Crazy Jane"; it shocked me.

The question mark and exclamation mark are placed inside the quotation marks if they are a part of the quotation; outside if they are not.

He asked, "Do you plan to attend the show?"

Could we describe the project as "essentially completed"?

Use *only one* terminal punctuation mark at end of sentences.

Who was it who said, "Know thyself"?

He frowned when she asked, "Why?"

Quiz

Review your knowledge of how to create good sentences with punctuation by taking the following quiz.

Directions: All internal punctuation has been omitted from the following sentences. Insert the appropriate punctuation to separate ideas, enclose incidental or parenthetical information, or emphasize certain elements of the sentence. The sentences could form a connected paragraph. The context will help you to decide what punctuation is needed. Some sentences may not require any additional punctuation.

1. In the United States legal system courts handle two kinds of cases.

2. Criminal cases involve violations of laws civil cases involve a private party with a claim against another party.

3. These parties may be individuals businesses organizations or government entities.

4. The party that believes it has been wronged asks the court for a remedy.

5. Damages the payment of money is one possible remedy.

6. Another remedy called an injunction forbids certain actions by the party at fault.

7. When the dispute involves a contract the court can order either party to comply with the contract's terms.

8. The court may declare the contract invalid or it may modify the contract's terms.

9. In some criminal cases the United States Supreme Court is asked to decide if a conviction violated the United States Constitution.

10. Clarence Earl Gideon a poor man living in Florida argued that his conviction of a felony was unconstitutional.

11. He had asked the Florida judge to appoint a lawyer but the judge had refused to do so.

12. The court had become increasingly concerned with the rights of two groups minorities and the poor.

13. On March 18 1963 the United States Supreme Court ruled that poor criminal defendants in state courts must be provided with attorneys.

Answers and Explanations

Added punctuation is in bold type so that you can see the additions easily.

1. In the United States legal system, courts handle two kinds of cases.

   Introductory prepositional phrases should be followed by a comma.

2. Criminal cases involve violations of laws; civil cases involve a private party with a claim against another party.

   Use a semi-colon to separates two independent clauses if their relationship is clear without the use of a conjunction.

3. These parties may be individuals, businesses, organizations, or government entities.

   In a series with a connective joining the last two items, the use of a comma before the connective is preferred usage.

4. The party that believes it has been wronged asks the court for a remedy.

   That believes it has been wronged is essential to the meaning of the sentence. Thus, it is a restrictive clause, and it is not set off by commas.

5. Damages, the payment of money, is one possible remedy.

   Non-restrictive appositives are set off by commas.

6. Another remedy (called an injunction) forbids certain actions by the party at fault.

   Parentheses indicate the enclosed element is loosely connected to the main idea of the sentence.

7. When the dispute involves a contract, the court can order either party to comply with the contract's terms.

An introductory adverbial clause is set off from the rest of the sentence, even when it is restrictive.

8. The court may declare the contract invalid, or it may modify the contract's terms.

To show a close relationship between clauses, use a comma and a coordinating conjunction.

9. In some criminal cases, the United States Supreme Court is asked to decide if a conviction violated the United States Constitution.

Introductory prepositional phrases should be followed by a comma.

10. Clarence Earl Gideon, a poor man living in Florida, argued that his conviction of a felony was unconstitutional.

Non-restrictive phrases are set off by commas.

11. He had asked the Florida judge to appoint a lawyer, but the judge had refused to do so.

To show a close relationship between clauses, use a comma and a coordinating conjunction.

12. The court had become increasingly concerned with the rights of two groups: minorities and the poor.

Use a colon after an expression that introduces a list, an explanation, or a quotation.

13. On March 18, 1963, the United States Supreme Court ruled that poor criminal defendants in state courts must be provided with attorneys.

Use commas to separate the parts of dates and to separate the date from the balance of the sentence.

9
COMMON USAGE ERRORS

Words and phrases that sound alike are frequently misused. Sometimes the error occurs because the writer does not know which spelling conveys the intended meaning. However, a spelling check on a word processor or computer will not reveal the error. Therefore, documents must be carefully proofread to avoid these errors. Part A contains expressions, words, and phrases that are frequently confused.

As we saw in Chapter 7, an idiom is a form of wording that cannot be explained by the rules of the grammar of a language. Idioms are specific to their native speakers. Americans, for example, *take a vacation*, while the British *go on holiday*. Americans ask *"how are you?"*; the French idiom with the same meaning would be translated literally as *"how do you go?"*. The most confusing idioms are prepositional. Nothing in logic or English grammar explains why we *agree to* doing something, but we *agree with* an idea. Part B contains a list of prepositional idioms.

Part A

1. **accept/except**
   To *accept* is to receive willingly; to *except* is to omit or exclude.

   I am pleased to accept this award.
   Everyone is going except you.

2. **adapt/adopt**
   To *adapt* is to change something; to *adopt* is to make something one's own.

   He was unable to adapt himself to the increased responsibility.
   The company wanted to adopt new marketing plans.

3. **adverse/averse**
   Adverse means strongly opposed to something; *averse* is merely reluctant.

   She is adverse to increased government spending.
   He is averse to making public appearances.

4. **affect/effect**
   This is an extremely common error. As a noun, *affect* is used in psychology to refer to feeling or emotion rather than thoughts or ideas. An *effect* is a result. To *affect* (verb) is to influence or change. To *effect*, which is much less common as a verb, means to bring about or to execute.

   The patient's *affect* was changed by anti-depressant medication.
   An *effect* of the medication was relief from depression.

   High unemployment rates *affected* the budget deficit.
   The governor *effected* the changes in tax rates.

5. **allude/elude**
   Allude is an indirect reference to; *elude* is to evade or escape from.

   I will try to allude to your contribution during my talk.
   He was able to elude the police for a week.

6. **allusion/illusion**
   An *allusion* is an indirect reference; an *illusion* is the act of deceiving the eye or mind.

   The story contains allusions to events during the Depression.
   Houdini created the illusion that he escaped from a locked trunk.

7. **alternate/alternative**
   An *alternate* is a substitute and also means every other; *alternative* is a selection of two choices.

   He was the alternate quarterback on alternate Sundays.
   Using Kareem or Shaq as center were the coach's only alternatives.

8. **amount/number**
   Amount applies to quantities that are measured; *number* is

applied to quantities that are counted.

She has a large amount of money in her account.
He invited a number of people to the party.

9. **appraise/apprise**
Appraise is to judge the value of something; *apprise* is to inform.

The jeweler appraised the bracelet at over $2,000.
When apprised of the value, she was surprised.

10. **any/either**
Any is used when there are three or more choices; *either* is a choice between one of two.

Sit in either (one or the other) chair.
Pick any seat (of all of them here) you wish.

11. **avert/avoid**
Avert is to turn away from; *avoid* is to keep away from.

He averted his eyes from the accident scene.
I want you to avoid gambling with company money.

12. **award/reward**
An *award is* usually given by a jud*ge*; a *reward* is received for service done.

She received the award for most sales during the year.
The man was given a reward for returning the lost painting.

13. **bad/badly**
The word *bad* is an adjective; *badly* is an adverb.

He felt bad after eating the cake.
He felt badly about not leaving any cake for anyone.

14. **beside/besides**
Beside means next to; *besides* means in addition to.

He stood beside the tree.
Besides me, you are her only other friend.

15. between/among

Usually, *between* refers to two: *among* refers to more than two.

She stood between her two children.
He stood proudly among his entire family.

16. bring/take

You *bring* something toward the person speaking and *take* something away from the person speaking.

Bring that book to me (over here).
Take this fork to her (over there).

17. bunch/crowd

Bunch is a collection of inanimate things; *crowd* is a number of people gathered together.

Here is a bunch of flowers.
Tom was lost in a crowd of spectators.

18. Calvary/cavalry

The first, *Calvary*, is the name of the place of the Crucifixion. *Cavalry* is the military on horseback.

Their first stop on the tour was Calvary.
Tennyson could hear the bugles of the cavalry coming over the hill.

19. capital/capitol

Capital means money or assets; *capitol* is a building where a state or national government is located.

Kristina had enough capital to expand her business.
Millions of people visit the state capitol every year.

20. censor/censure

To *censor* is to change or ban a book, movie, or other work; to *censure* is to criticize or condemn.

The committee decided to censor the novel, and remove it from the high school library.
D.H Lawrence's work was censured and not permitted to be printed in Great Britain.

21. childish/childlike

One who *is childish* is usually immature or foolish; one who is *childlike* is innocent and pure.

They were embarrassed by his childish actions.
His childlike manner convinced us he was sincere.

22. climactic/climatic

Climactic refers to the climax. (You can remember it by the hard "c" sound before the "t.") *Climatic* has to do with the weather.

She walked out at a climactic moment in the film.
The climatic conditions are unbearable.

23. complement/compliment

Here is one of the most common errors. *Complement* means to complete. Remember it by the first "e" in complete. *Compliment* is an expression of praise. Try to keep in mind the "i" of praise to remember the "i" in compliment.

The wine complemented the roast perfectly.
We complimented the chef on the fine meal.

24. conscious/conscience

One's *conscious* or aware of one's knowledge of one's self and one's surroundings; one's *conscience* is the knowledge of moral values.

I was conscious that there were other people listening.
His conscience made him admit his errors.

25. credible/creditable/credulous

Credible means believable; *creditable* means worth honor or esteem; *credulous* means believing too easily.

Her excuse was credible and they believed her.
His creditable actions on the football team were praised by all.
He was too credulous and fell into his trap.

26. custom/habit

A *habit* is a continuing action, and a *custom* is what is derived from habits, usually in groups.

Mick had a bad habit of biting his fingernails.
It was their custom to eat dinner early.

27. dairy/diary

These words are often misused because we don't look closely at them. A *dairy* is where cows live; a *diary* is a book to record thoughts, and activities.

Farmer Schmidt kept all the records of the dairy in a diary.

28. delusion/illusion

A *delusion is* a continual inaccurate belief; an *illusion* is an inaccurate perception of reality.

She was under the delusion that she was a rock star.
The mirror created an illusion of space in the room.

29. discover/invent

Discover means to locate something that had been there all along, while *invent* means to create something that had not already existed.

Although Columbus is credited with discovering America, Native Americans had been living there for several thousand years.
The Apple computer was invented very young men.

30. distinctive/distinguished

Distinctive means making a difference by setting apart, and *distinguished* means prominent or famous.

We can easily spot the team members in their distinctive uniforms.
The senators turned in their seats to look at the distinguished visitors who entered the chamber.

31. economic/economical

Economic refers to the study of the subject of economics or relating to an economy; *economical* means being frugal instead of wasteful.

The country's economic problems were extremely deep rooted.
It is more economical for you to travel by train than by plane to your destination.

32. **efficacy/efficiency**

   Efficacy refers to the power to produce a specific effect, while *efficiency* refers to the ability to produce a desired result with the least amount of effort.

   The efficacy of the engine was proven when the results of all tests were successful.
   Emily was hired because of her efficiency in scheduling meetings.

33. **emigrate/immigrate**

   Emigrate refers to leaving one's country to establish residency in another, and *immigrate* refers to the act of entering a new country.

   Soo's ancestors emigrated from China.
   It had been their lifelong dream to immigrate to America.

34. **eminent/imminent**

   Eminent means of highest merit, while *imminent* means likely to occur soon.

   The auditorium was filled by people who had come to hear the eminent physician speak.
   Spectators lined the sidewalks, anticipating the imminent arrival of the parade.

35. **ensure/insure/assure**

   Ensure means to make sure and certain; *insure* means to guarantee against harm; and *assure* means to provide confidence.

   The insurance agent assured his clients that the best way for them to ensure their minds was by insuring their property with Stone Casualty Company.

36. **enthuse**

   Do not confuse enthuse with enthusiasm. Although *enthuse* is the verbal form of *enthusiasm*, it is not considered good grammatical usage.

   Instead of saying … "The rousing performance enthused the audience."
   Say … "The rousing performance stirred the audience."

37. famous/notorious

Famous refers to having a celebrated, well-known reputation. while *notorious* refers to a reputation that is negative, unpleasing.

Raymond Massey was famous for his portrayal of Lincoln.
The Purple Gang was notorious for their robberies.

38. fatal/ fateful

Fatal means resulting in destruction or death, while *fateful* refers to a predictable outcome of significance.

On the anniversary of this fateful day, the President memorialized the names of the victims of the fatal victims of the attack.

39. fewer/less

Fewer refers to people or things that can be counted, while *less* refers to a smaller quantity.

We took in less funds this year because fewer people attended our concerts.

40. flaunt/flout

Flaunt means to act in such a way as to show off, and *flout* means to insult.

Egon flaunted his promotion by having his title placed on his office door.
It is poor sportsmanship for the winners to flout the losers.

41. formally (formal)/formerly (former)

Formally refers to conventional, formal ways; and *formerly* refers to events which occurred previously, articles once owned, or people with whom one used to associate.

Her former husband was quite formal in his attire.

42. hanged/hung

The meaning of both words is the same; what differs is the fact that *hanged* refers to animate objects, *hung* refers to inanimate objects.

Out West, bandits were hanged for disobeying certain laws.
They hung the Halloween decorations on the front windows.

43. imaginary/imaginative

Imaginary means existing only in the imagination, unreal; *imaginative* refers to being inventive, creative.

The child played quietly in the attic with imaginary friend.
Mr. Roberts' imaginative stories delighted the children.

44. immoral/amoral

Immoral means corrupt, bad, sinful, while *amoral* refers to an act with neither moral nor immoral significance.

Depictions of immoral behavior in films have become quite common.
Eating dinner a midnight is an amoral act.

45. immunity/impunity

Immunity refers to being safe from injury; *impunity* means to be free of punishment.

This vaccine shot will enable the children to get an immunity to whooping cough.
After the teacher left, the schoolchildren ran with impunity throughout the room.

46. imply/infer

Imply is an action done by the originator of a message and means to hint at something, while *infer* is an action done by the recipient of a message and means to derive or deduce a meaning from the message.

You restlessness implies that you want to leave.
What I infer from your behavior is that we should leave now.

47. incredible/incredulous

Note that these words are the opposite in meaning from credible/credulous. *Incredible* means beyond belief, and *incredulous* refers to being skeptical.

His explanation of the accident was incredible.
She gave him an incredulous look when he tried to explain the situation to her.

48. **ingenious/ingenuous**
Ingenious means skillful, intelligent; *ingenuous* means innocent and, also, frank and honest.

She solved the problem with an ingenious plan.
He is so ingenuous that he cannot believe anyone could ever mislead him.

49. **innate/inert**
Innate refers to natural and inborn, while *inert* means having no motion, lifeless.

She has an innate ability to handle most mechanical jobs.
The deer, struck by a car, lay inert on the side of the road where it had fallen.

50. **kind of/sort of**
Not to be confused with rather/somewhat. *Kind of* refers to a type of, and *sort of* refers to a category of.

That kind of dog is hardly ever seen around here.
What sort of casserole would you prefer I bring?

51. **like/as**
Both words are used to show comparisons, but *like* is used in phrases, *as* is used in clauses.

He ate like a horse.
He lives as if he were rich.

52. **the number/a number**
The number refers to verbs in the singular, and *a number* refers to verbs in the plural.

The number of rooms in this house is thirty.
A number of cookies are still left in the cookie jar.

53. **perpetrate/perpetuate**
Perpetrate means to commit an action, usually associated with committing a hoax or a crime, while *perpetuate* means to continue something forever.

The criminal conspiracy perpetrated fraud against the company's investors.

The striking employees complained that the factory perpetuated the unsafe conditions of the machines by refusing to repair them.

54. persecute/prosecute

Persecute means to persistently harass, while *prosecute* means to carry on a lawsuit in trial against someone.

The children persecuted the new student because he was very short.
Al Capone was prosecuted by the IRS for tax evasion.

55. personal/personnel

Personal refers to a person, and *personnel* refers to any group of people employed in one place.

The manager's personal opinion is that personnel in the company should have three weeks of paid vacation each year.

56. phenomenon/phenomena

Phenomenon is the singular form and *phenomena* is the plural form of the word that means something out of the ordinary.

The blizzard in Florida was a phenomenon.
The astronauts observed the phenomena on the earth, from space.

57. practicable/practical

Practicable refers to objects and means able to be done, or usable; *practical* refers to the usefulness of doing something.

It is not considered practicable to live on Mars, but maybe someday scientists will find a way for people to do so.
We often follow our attorney's advice because it is so practical.

58. precede/proceed

Precede refers to placement of ideas or objects before the rest, while *proceed* means to continue.

Movie theaters precede the feature film with previews of new films.
They proceeded with their plans for a picnic despite the threat of rain.

59. **prescribe/proscribe**
Prescribe means to recommend directions, and *proscribe* means to banish or prohibit something.

Each of the three doctors prescribed the same method of treatment for his ailment.
The sign states that eating, drinking, and smoking are proscribed in the auditorium.

60. **principal/principle**
Principal is both an adjective, meaning main, and a noun, meaning the leader; *principle* refers to a fundamental rule.

The principal purpose of this meeting is to establish a principle of conduct for all students at school.

61. **remediable/remedial**
Remediable means capable of being fixed or cured, and *remedial* refers to having a remedy or cure.

To find out if a used car is in remediable condition, take it to a mechanic to get an appraisal.
Remedial therapy may help victims of a stroke.

62. **respectfully/respectively**
Respectfully means with courtesy, with good behavior; *respectively* refers to the order that things are given.

The children were taught to speak to adults respectfully.
Thanksgiving, Christmas, and New Year's Eve occur within the last six weeks of the year respectively.

63. **turbid/turgid**
Turbid refers to dense, foggy conditions; and *turgid* means bloated, swollen.

The airplane cannot take off until the skies are less turbid.
The turgid appearance of the patient's wrist indicates that it may be sprained.

64. **when/where**

Be careful not to mix up the use of *when* or *where* in a clause. For example: do not say ... "a ballet is when dancers perform..." but say ... "a ballet is a type of dance in which dancers ..." Do not say ... "camping is where people ...", but say ... "camping is an activity that involves living out of doors ..."

Part B—Prepositional Idioms

1.	accede *to*	We cannot *accede to* your request for an extension of time.
2.	accessory *of*	He was an *accessory of* the criminal.
3.	accessory *to*	She was an *accessory to* the act.
4.	accommodate *to*	He finds it hard to *accommodate* himself *to* new situations. (changed conditions)
5.	accommodate *with*	We *accommodated* her *with* a loan of five dollars.
6.	accompany *by*	He was *accompanied by* his uncle. (a person)
7.	accompany *with*	The letter was *accompanied with* an affidavit. (a thing)
8.	accord *in*	The committee members *accord in* their decisions.
9.	accord *to*	There shall be *accorded to* each person what is earned.
10.	accord *with*	I am in *accord with* the findings.
11.	accountable *for*	The President is *accountable for* his actions.
12.	accountable *to*	I am *accountable to* the dean for my actions.
13.	accused *by*	He was *accused by* the plaintiff of having stolen a car.
14.	accused *of*	She was *accused of* perjury.

15. acquiesce *in* — The manager *acquiesced in* the decision.

16. acquit *of* — Simpson was *acquitted of* the crime.

17. acquit *with* — She *acquitted* herself *with* honor.

18. adapted *for* — The English cookbook was modified and *adapted for* an American audience.

19. adapted *from* — The movie was *adapted from* the book.

20. adapted *to* — He finds it difficult to *adapt to* new procedures.

21. adequate *for* — Her salary was not *adequate for* her needs.

22. adequate *to* — His ability was *adequate to* the job.

23. adverse *to* — The politician was not *adverse to* discussing the compromise.

24. averse *to* — He was not *averse to* hard work.

25. advise *of* — The employees were *advised of* the new regulations.

26. affix *to* — A label was *affixed to* the container.

27. agree *in* — We *agree in* principle with those who favor the plan.

28. agree *on* — They cannot *agree on* the new plan.

29. agree *to* — They state that they *agree to* the compromise.

30. agree *with* — They both *agree with* us in theory.

31. amenable *to* — She was *amenable to* our argument.

32. analogous *to* — This situation is *analogous to* the one we faced last year.

33. annoy *by* — The teacher was *annoyed by* the frequent interruptions.

34. annoy *with*   The observer notices that the teacher was *annoyed with* the student.

35. apparent *in*   His attitude is *apparent in* his actions.

36. apparent *to*   The trouble is *apparent to* everyone in the office.

37. append *to*   A rider was *appended to* the bill.

38. appreciation *for*   The student had a real *appreciation for* the arts.

39. appreciation *of*   She expressed *appreciation of* their hard work.

40. appreciative *of*   We are *appreciative of* their efforts.

41. authority *in*   Dr. Mohammed is an *authority in* her field.

42. authority *on*   Ms. Rodriguez is an *authority on* programming.

43. authority *to*   He has *authority to* sign this document.

44. basis *for*   The lawyer said they had a sound *basis for* agreement.

45. basis *in*   His argument has no *basis in* fact.

46. commensurate *with* Her salary was *commensurate with* her abilities.

47. comply *with*   We must *comply with* the leader's request.

48. concur *in*   We *concur in* the decision of the marketing committee.

49. concur *with*   One member did not *concur with* the others.

50. conform *to*   All students must *conform to* the regulations.

51. consist *in*   Kim's value *consists in* the ability to work

with others.

52.	consist *of*	The handbook *consists of* principles of supervision.
53.	consistent *in*	We should be *consistent in* applying the rules.
54.	consistent *with*	The mayor's actions are not *consistent with* statements made by assistants.
55.	correspond *to*	The description of the incident *corresponds to* what we thought happened.
56.	correspond *with*	She has been *corresponding with* her sister.
57.	demand *from*	What did he *demand from* them in payment?
58.	demand *of*	They have *demanded of* the company an accounting of funds.
59.	differ *from*	My estimate of the total damage *differs from* the insurance company's.
60.	differ *in*	We *differ in* our opinions on the matter.
61.	differ *on*	They *differed on* the amount to be paid.
62.	differ *with*	I *differ with* the coach about the method used to train the team.
63.	discrepancy *between*	There is *a discrepancy between* the two stories.
64.	discrepancy *in*	There is *a discrepancy in* this story.
65.	displeased *by*	The boss was *displeased by* the employee's conduct.
66.	displeased *with*	The teacher was *displeased with* the student.
67.	eligible *for*	Clancy is *eligible for* the job.
68.	eligible *to*	Everyone is *eligible to* apply for the job.
69.	equivalent *in*	Amy's office and mine are *equivalent in* size.

70.	equivalent *of*	This is the *equivalent of* a full payment.
71.	equivalent *to*	Each payment is *equivalent to* a week's salary.
72.	excepted *from*	They were *excepted from* further responsibility.
73.	excluded *from*	This package was *excluded from* your shipment.
74.	exempt *from*	This type of merchandise is *exempt from* sales tax.
75.	expect *from*	What return do you *expect from* your investment?
76.	expect *of*	What does the teacher *expect of* her students?
77.	familiar *to*	The name Kennedy is *familiar to* me.
78.	familiar *with*	Bond is quite *familiar with* the rules of the game.
79.	find *for*	The jury *found for* the defendant.
80.	furnish *to*	Adequate food was *furnished to* them.
81.	furnish *with*	Please *furnish us with* background information on this matter.
82.	habit *of*	She made a *habit of* walking early in the morning.
83.	identical *with*	That briefcase is *identical with* the one I own.
84.	identify *by*	The man was *identified by* the tattoo on his arm.
85.	identify *to*	The witness *identified* the suspect *to* this office.

86. identify *with*   King *identified with* the people he spoke for.

87. ignorant *of*   She was *ignorant of* her civil rights as a citizen.

88. improvement *in*   The *improvement in* his writing was very obvious.

89. improvement *on*   Austen's second novel was an *improvement on* the first.

90. inconsistent *in*   Duke was *inconsistent in* his training program.

91. inconsistent *with*   This is *inconsistent with* established policy.

92. infer *from*   We *infer from* his speech that the governor plans to run again next year.

93. influence *for*   Robinson's *influence* was always *for* harmony.

94. influence *by*   We were all *influenced by* the coach's speech.

95. influence *on (upon)*   The rumor of a management change had an *influence on* (upon) production.

96. influence *over*   Lincoln had a strong *influence over* his generals.

97. influence *with*   The publicity agent referred frequently to his *influence with* those in authority.

98. inform *of*   Supervisors should keep their subordinates *informed of* any changes in procedure.

99. inherent *in*   A capacity for growth is *inherent in* all people.

100. insert *in*   This phrase should be *inserted in* the speech.

101. intercede *for*	My mother *interceded for* me.
102. intercede *with*	The *politician interceded with* the authorities on in my behalf.
103. invest *in*	The broker said she had *invested* the money *in* stocks.
104. invest *with*	She was *invested with* full power to act.
105. irrelevant *to*	Your statement *is irrelevant to* our discussion.
106. irrespective *of*	They decided to let Bo play *irrespective of* the injury that might result.
107. liable *for*	He is *liable for* damages.
108. liable *to*	An employee is *liable to* an employer.
109. liberal *in*	Feinstein was very *liberal in* her views.
110. liberal *with*	Grandparents are *liberal with* praise for grandchildren.
111. necessity *for*	There is no *necessity for a* new initiative.
112. necessity *of*	We are faced with the *necessity of* reducing travel expenses.
113. oblivious *of*	He was *oblivious of* the effect that his poor manners had on his family.
114. precedent *for*	Is there a *precedent for* this action?
115. precedent *in*	The judge's decision established a *precedent in* law.
116. recompense *for*	He was fully *recompensed for* the time he spent on the work.
117. reconcile *to*	We have become *reconciled to* our fate.
118. reconcile *with*	Our views cannot be *reconciled with* theirs.

119. similarity *in*   I agree that there is much *similarity in* their appearance.

120. similarity *of*   The *similarity of* the names caused confusion.

121. similarity *to*   This copying machine shows a *similarity to* one I own.

122. talk *of*   The traveler *talked of* his experiences in many countries.

123. talk *to*   The lecturer *talked to* a large audience.

124. talk *with*   The driver *talked with* the passenger.

125. transfer *from*   He has been *transferred from* his former position.

126. transfer *to*   They *transferred* her *to* another department.

127. unequal *in*   The contestants were *unequal in* strength.

128. unequal *to*   He was *unequal to* the demands placed on him.

129. use *for*   She had no *use for* the extra copies of the memo.

130. use *of*   The athlete made good *use of* the opportunity.

131. wait *at*   I will *wait at* the back of the room until I can talk with the speaker.

132. wait *for*   He seemed to be *waiting for* someone.

133. wait *on (upon)*   This matter must *wait on* (upon) my leisure.

Quiz

This quiz will review you knowledge of words that are frequently confused.

Directions: Circle the correct word or phrase of the two choices in the parentheses.

1. Her job was not (affected/effected) by the company's decision to downsize.

2. What (affect/effect) will the decision have on the company's balance sheet?

3. Please keep the client (appraised/apprised) of the progress of the lawsuit.

4. Divide the credit for increased sales (among/between) the publicity and advertising departments.

5. Serena was (conscious/conscience) that her tennis outfit was sensational.

6. This week, the film attracted (fewer/less) viewers than it did last week.

7. The reader (implies/infers) the main idea although it is not stated explicitly.

8. (As/like) he should, the architect drew the plans with great care.

9. The film was edited and (adapted for/adapted to) television audiences.

10. Huck Finn did not want to (conform to/conform with) Aunt Polly's rules.

11. This copying machine's features (differ from/differ with) the features of that machine.

12. Readers (identify to/identify with) the main character of the novel.

13. Hypocrites' words are (inconsistent to/inconsistent with) their actions.

14. Disliking sweets, she was (oblivious of/oblivious to) the delights of chocolate fudge.

15. Although their prices differ, there is much (similarity in/similarity to) the picture quality of these DVD players.

Answers and Explanations

Note: Because idioms are not logical, no explanation is possible for some of the idiom items. The correct answer is the way the idiom is used in standard written English.

1. Her job was not *affected* by the company's decision to downsize.

   Affect is the verb meaning to influence or to change.

2. What *effect* will the decision have on the company's balance sheet?

   Effect is the noun which means a result.

3. Please keep the client *apprised* of the progress of the lawsuit.

   Apprise is the verb that means to inform.

4. Divide the credit for increased sales *between* the publicity and advertising departments.

   Use *between* when referring to only two items.

5. Serena was *conscious* that her tennis outfit was sensational.

   Conscious is the noun meaning aware of.

6. This week, the film attracted *fewer* viewers than it did last week.

   Use *fewer* as the adjective to describe people or things that can be counted.

7. The reader *infers* the main idea although it is not stated explicitly.

    To *infer* is the action by the receiver of a message.

8. *As* he should, the architect drew the plans with great care.

    Use *as* in modifying clauses.

9. The film was edited and *adapted for* television audiences.

10. Huck Finn did not want to *conform to* Aunt Polly's rules.

11. This copying machine's features *differ from* the features of that machine.

    Differ from indicates a contrast. *Differ with* means to disagree with.

12. Readers *identify with* the main character of the novel.

13. Hypocrites' words are *inconsistent with* their actions.

14. Disliking sweets, she was *oblivious of* the delights of chocolate fudge.

15. Although their prices differ, there is much *similarity in* the picture quality of these DVD players.

    Similarity in suggests two things are alike. *Similarity to* indicates a comparison of two things that seem different.

INDEX